A Compassionate Approach to Gender and Development

A Compassionate Approach to Gender and Development

From Local Stories to Global Visions

First Edition

Ranjeeta Basu

California State University—San Marcos

cognella®
SAN DIEGO

Bassim Hamadeh, CEO and Publisher
Mieka Portier, Senior Acquisitions Editor
Carrie Baarns, Manager, Revisions and Author Care
Michelle Piehl, Senior Project Editor
Susana Christie, Senior Developmental Editor
Jeanine Rees, Production Editor
Jess Estrella, Senior Graphic Designer
Alexa Lucido, Licensing Manager
Stephanie Adams, Senior Marketing Program Manager
Natalie Piccotti, Director of Marketing
Kassie Graves, Senior Vice President, Editorial
Jamie Giganti, Director of Academic Publishing

Printed in the United States of America.

Contents

Preface

In this book we will consider gender and development issues within a social justice framework that is grounded in compassion. I have been studying and teaching in this field for over 25 years and every time I teach courses in this area, I am able to see things I haven't seen before and, as a result, think about things in a new way. I grew up in Mumbai, India, in a middle-class family. Most of the women in my family had access to education. My mother was a high school teacher and continues to be my role model. My aunt Supriya Roy impressed upon me the importance of scholarship and research. I attended St. Xavier's College and was inspired by my first economics teacher, Brother Agnelo, to study economics because he focused on the reasons some people had access to material resources and others did not. I wanted to attend graduate school to explore these questions in greater depth, and I ended up in the United States. I returned home almost every year to visit my family but also to remain connected to these questions that inspired me as a young adult. I have one biological daughter, but also hundreds of sons and daughters and those with other gender identities that I have had the joy of teaching and learning from over the years and who remind me every day why asking these questions is important. As you open the pages of this book and we embark on this journey together, I urge you to open your mind and open your heart and enjoy the experience of exploring new thoughts, new ideas, and new dialogues. I hope that this book will help you to better understand these issues and better frame your own lived experiences within a broader context. Reading this book will help us

- Understand historical legacies and systems of oppression based on gender, class, race, and national identity in a global context using economic tools of analysis.
- Analyze the economic relationship between patriarchy and capital accumulation and the way in which these two economic systems have perpetuated oppression of women and other marginalized groups domestically and globally.
- Identify the ways these systems of oppression continue to manifest themselves in the economic lives of women, men, and children in the workplace and in the household today.
- Identify the ways in which a global public health crisis (specifically the COVID-19 pandemic) has exacerbated the economic inequalities between men and women in the workplace and in the household.

- Identify the ways in which climate change has exacerbated the economic inequalities between men and women in the workplace and in the household.
- Develop respect, empathy, and compassion for difference in a global context.
- Develop the ability to advocate and be an agent of change for global justice and gender equity.

Gender and development is an interdisciplinary field with its roots in the social sciences. Although economics is the focus of this book, political science, sociology, anthropology, and history are all invoked to assist in the analysis of the critical issues facing women in development. This is a broad field, and this book will not cover all of the richness that this field of study has to offer; this book will hopefully spark your interest toward further research and study. In this book, we will focus on the following four overarching questions:

- How and in what historical context are the terms "development" and "Third World women" socially constructed?
- Why and in what way can gender analysis be used to reexamine development theories and policies?
- What is the relationship between patriarchy and capital accumulation? Who gains from this system and why?
- How can we use this analysis to imagine and reconstruct alternative visions of the future that are grounded in compassion?

Chapter 1

Introduction to Concepts of Social Justice and Compassion

> I am no longer accepting the things I cannot change. I am changing the things I cannot accept.
>
> —Angela Davis, American political activist, philosopher, and educator

From Local Stories to Global Visions

Countless local stories and global statistics demonstrate with heartbreaking clarity that women produce most of the food in the world but are more likely to be malnourished. Women are more likely to have primary responsibility for the household but less likely to own a home. Women provide most of the care services in the world but are less likely to receive care. Instead of receiving care, women are more likely to face domestic abuse, sexual harassment, and physical violence. These are not uncommon occurrences but instead the norm. In fact, there is no country in the world that treats women as well as it treats men.

Invitation to reflect: Take a moment to re-read the sentences above and reflect on which of them resonates with you the most and why.

Introduction

Our current experience of the pandemic has not only revealed these inequalities but also worsened them in many cases. As an educator, I was able to keep my job and continue teaching in a virtual environment, but for many women around the world that was not the case. Women's overrepresentation in sectors such as healthcare and social services (more than 70%), which were deemed as *essential* during the pandemic, put them at greater risk of exposure to the virus. With the shutdown of schools, childcare centers, and elderly care services, much of the care work shifted into the home and increased hours fell disproportionately on women. Pre-COVID-19, roughly 76% of the total amount of unpaid care work was done by women. During the pandemic, this imbalance in unpaid care work worsened. Early worldwide assessments by the International Labour Organization (ILO) indicate that women are spending on average 30 hours per week on childcare alone since the pandemic began. With no children living at home, I did not spend additional hours in childcare. But I have heard from women with small children about the many hours they spent and continue to spend facilitating online learning for their children in addition to cooking and cleaning for the family. For example, many middle-class families in Mumbai have domestic help, most of whom are migrant women. The sudden lockdown precipitated by COVID-19 meant that many of these women couldn't go to work and had to return to their villages without transportation, without social protections, without health care or paid employment. The work that they were doing in the home shifted to the women in these households, many of whom had to give up or reduce their hours of paid employment. In the labor market globally, women lost 54 million jobs during 2019 and 2020. While men will have recouped much of the job loss they experienced by the end of 2021, women will have fallen short by 13 million jobs. According to UN Women's projections, 47 million additional women will experience extreme poverty by the end of 2021.

Women are also more affected by global climate change and yet are not included in decision-making and agenda-setting in this area. It is now more imperative than ever before for us to understand the complexity of these issues and work together to create a world where people have the same opportunity to thrive and to participate in shaping the future that we all face—regardless of their gender identity. The unprecedented upheaval in our economic and social structures over the last 18 months has had a devastating effect on gender equality, but it has also provided us with an opportunity to envision a different path forward. We have experienced this crisis together, and we need to come out of it together. Toward this end, UN Women released a bold new feminist vision for social justice and sustainability on September 16, 2021. It addresses the triple crises of job loss, climate change, and a fractured care economy (UN Women, 2021).

In this chapter, we start by establishing a common understanding of the concepts of social justice, oppression, and compassion, which we can then apply to the specific topic of gender and development. We will also understand why compassion is necessary for us to build a more just and sustainable world. This chapter also provides evidence of existing gender disparities in jobs, education, income, and poverty and how they not only lead to worse outcomes for women and children, but they also lead to lower GDP and productivity.

What Is Social Justice?

Any social structure that unequally confers resources, opportunities, and decision-making power to some groups of people over other groups of people is socially unjust and needs to be challenged and dismantled in order to achieve social justice. Social justice can be defined both in terms of processes and in terms of outcomes. **Social justice requires that all people have the same rights and are treated fairly such that it leads to equitable opportunities and equitable outcomes for all.** In this book our focus will be on gender equality, which requires that people regardless of their gender identity have the same rights, opportunities, and access to resources, while recognizing that other social identities such as race/ethnicity, citizenship, class, sexual orientation are considered as well to ensure that *intersectionality* has been incorporated into our analysis.

Crenshaw (1991) defines "intersectionality" as the lens through which one can understand the ways in which multiple sources of power that arise from different social identities intersect and collide with each other.

Equitable opportunities include access to (1) high-quality education and well-paid employment; (2) civic and political participation; and (3) universal health care and social services. In the area of employment, roughly 63% of working aged women participate in the paid labor force globally as compared to 94% of working aged men. In the area of education, while we have achieved global gender parity at the primary education level, only 79 women for every 100 men complete secondary school in low-income countries. As a result, the adult literacy rate in low-income countries is 54% among women as compared to 69% for men. In the area of political participation, UN Women reports that, globally, women in parliamentary forms of government have doubled over the last 25 years from 11% in 1995 to 26% in 2021, indicating that we have made some progress. However, women's access remains much lower than men's participation in this area. Most of the gap is seen at senior levels of leadership. All these areas are connected to each other in that lower access to education often translates into lack of access to well-paid jobs, which in turn affects access to social services and health care. Table 1 summarizes the latest ILO estimates of access to social services and social protections, including unemployment benefits, child and family benefits, and old-age pensions.

Table 1 Proportion of population with comprehensive legal social protection coverage

Region	Female	Male	Total
World	30.6%	34.3%	26.5%
Africa	7.3%	10.8%	3.9%
Americas	42.1%	45.3%	37.7%
Arab States	24.2%	36.1%	8.6%
Asia and the Pacific	29.0%	32.9%	24.7%
Europe & Central Asia	52.7%	55.0%	49.7%

Source: World Social Protection Report 2020–2022, ILO

As a result of these very low levels of social protection, people in most countries around the world, especially women, were hard hit by the pandemic. Despite the progress we have made, we were not prepared for a crisis of this magnitude.

Social justice is not only about access to opportunities and resources, but it is also about outcomes. Equitable outcomes imply distributive justice where income and productive assets are distributed fairly and equitably, especially for those who have the least (Rawls 1971, 2001). UN Women reports that, globally, women earn 16% less than men, which means that they earn 84 cents for every dollar earned by men. While there are variations by country, there is no country that has managed to close the gender gap in wages. It is important to note that equity does not always mean equality. Equality assumes that everyone started at the same point with identical resources and initial endowments and therefore fair treatment implies that everyone is treated in the same way. Equity recognizes that everyone does not start from the same point and therefore some might need more support to have the same opportunity to thrive as others who have access to more resources. For example, people who are differently abled (some countries prefer to use the term "disabled") might need different levels of support to be able to enjoy the same opportunity to thrive, leading to national policies on accessibility.

Fair and equitable social processes ensure that all people have equal opportunity to participate in determining not only their own lives, but also in determining group norms, institutions, and policies. Everyone feels like their voices are heard, they are acknowledged, and their contributions valued and compensated fairly. Equitable social processes also recognize and appreciate the immense diversity in human expression, ideas, needs, endowments, cultures, values, and contributions. Each of us has something to contribute and something to learn from each other that is unique and valuable. Not only are women worse off when they are not at the table, but all of us are worse off because we are deprived of the diversity of ideas and expertise that women's voices would provide. For example, in the last 30 years only 13% of negotiators of peace have been women, even after the UN Security Council passed a resolution in 2000 that recognized that war affects women differently from men and resolved to include more women in peace negotiations.

Invitation to reflect: Take a moment to reflect on how peace negotiations might be different if more women were at the table.

Measuring the Global Gender Gap

The global gender gap index is a measure that combines four dimensions—economic participation, political participation, educational attainment, and health and survival—to give us an overall measure of gender equality across 156 countries. The index measures progress made toward closing the gender gap on a scale of 0 to 100. The Global Gender Gap Report 2021 suggests that we have lost ground during the pandemic in terms of achieving gender equality, from 69% in 2019 to 68% in 2021. As a result, it will now take us 135 years to achieve global gender parity as compared to the 99 years as projected in 2020. The largest gap is found in political participation with only 22% of the gender gap closed in 2021, down 2.4% from 2019. At the current rate it will take us 145 years to close the gender gap in political participation. In 81 countries there has never been a woman head of state; including in the United States. Greater political participation by women is key to bringing about social change especially via legislative processes. The second largest gap is found in economic participation, which is at 58%, a marginal improvement over last year, although the impact of the pandemic is not fully reflected in these numbers yet. At this rate it will take us 267 years to achieve gender parity. Much of the gap is found in senior leadership positions. For example, only 8% of CEOs of Fortune 500 companies are women. The gender gaps in educational attainment (95%) and health and survival (96%) are almost closed, but significant variations across countries need to be addressed. Iceland remains the most gender equal country in the world at 89.2%, followed closely by other Scandinavian countries. Afghanistan is the least gender equal country in the world at 44%. The data clearly reveals that women and men do not have the same opportunity to thrive in most parts of the world, unequivocally confirming gender inequality and oppression as a global social justice issue. Gender equality would not only give women greater opportunities to thrive, more choices, and more agency, but it would also benefit all of society by leading to accelerated economic growth, reduced poverty, and better health and educational outcomes for women and children.

What Is Oppression?

Social injustice is initiated and perpetuated by systems of oppression and exploitation. **An oppressive structure systematically confers rights and privileges on the dominant group, which benefits from and has power over the subordinate group. Members of the subordinate group are systematically denied the autonomy and capacity to thrive, and their contributions are marginalized and appropriated by the dominant group.** Indian economist, philosopher, and Nobel Prize winner Amartya Sen (2010) argues that social justice expands capabilities, which are defined as the freedom to choose the kind of lives that people value. When women are systematically denied the same capabilities that are afforded to men, then such a situation is oppressive and socially unjust. For example, with the Taliban returning to power in Afghanistan this year, women have been denied the same rights enjoyed by men. Hence their capabilities and their life opportunities have been diminished.

The concept of oppression has several defining characteristics. According to American sociologists and educators Adams and Bell (2016), oppression is characterized as restrictive, pervasive, and cumulative. Oppression is restrictive because it prevents access to opportunities and resources or denies the subordinate group basic human rights enjoyed by the dominant group. For example, women might be denied access to education or might be discouraged from entering certain fields. These restrictions, especially when imposed and experienced at an early age, dramatically reduce possibilities for thriving and surviving and are a loss not just for the person experiencing it but also for all of humanity. We are all worse off when women are not able to reach their full potential because we lose all the contributions that women would have made. Education also leads to better understanding, sound decision-making, and greater civic engagement.

For a phenomenon to be called oppressive, it must also be pervasive. In other words, we are not talking about one or two cases of someone being denied access to a resource. We are talking about entire groups of people or groups of nations being denied access to opportunities or resources in a systematic way over long periods of time in history. Historical legacies, institutions, laws, economic policies, social norms, cultural and symbolic representations all work together to reinforce systems of oppression such that they pervade every aspect of society. Just like a fish who doesn't know that it is wet, oppression can often become so pervasive that we don't question it or even see it as something that can be changed.

Oppression is also cumulative in that one form of oppression often leads to another form of oppression, creating interlocking layers of oppression that bind and reinforce each other. For example, women being denied access to education might mean that they don't have access to good quality jobs, which might mean they don't have access to loans, which, in turn, means they don't have access to housing and leads to multiple forms of oppression that are all connected to each other. This makes it harder to break the cycle.

Oppression is based on categories that are socially constructed to create power hierarchies. For example, a characteristic such as gender is used to divide people into two distinct categories of men and women with certain assigned traits and social roles. These are reinforced through the socialization process to create a socially constructed narrative about the supposed superiority of one gender over the other, i.e., men are strong and women are weak. People are then treated differently based on their gender and given differential access to resources and jobs. When people don't conform to these rigid categories, they face shaming, censure, and discrimination. The dominant group uses the power hierarchy that is created to oppress and exploit the subordinate groups. Resulting inequities in jobs and incomes are then explained away as natural or biological versus being socially constructed. Over time these socially constructed categories and the accompanying power hierarchies become so embedded in our social structures that members of the dominant group enjoy privileged access to resources and opportunities without even being aware of it. For example, many men may not be aware that they have male privilege because they have never known what it feels like to not have those privileges.

Invitation to reflect: Take a moment to reflect on when you first became aware of your own gender identity and how it made you feel.

Oppression is often perpetuated and reinforced through hegemony and internalization of one's dominant or subordinate position. **"Hegemony" refers to the normalization of oppression as the natural or inevitable way such that alternative ways are marginalized and rendered unthinkable.** Hegemony operates through institutional processes and norms. It also operates through cultural and symbolic channels as *dominant narratives* that legitimize certain ways of knowing and certain ways of looking at the world. Any attempt to question or challenge the dominant narrative is dismissed as abnormal or irrational or ignorant. Internalization of one's own subordinate position not only reduces the possibility of challenging the dominant narrative, but it is ultimately a self-fulfilling mechanism. For example, if a girl child is repeatedly told that she is not capable of mathematical analysis, then she might internalize that false narrative and not even try to learn mathematics, thereby reinforcing the stereotype.

It is important to understand how systems of oppression work so that we can consciously and deliberately take action to dismantle them. If systems of oppression can be socially constructed, they can also be deconstructed. Oppression diminishes our collective and individual humanity. When we see others simply as means to an end, we are unable to experience the richness of social connection that we are capable of and need to have to thrive and survive as a species. We must believe that slowly, but surely, one step at a time, we can challenge oppression and ultimately bring about structural changes that move us toward social justice. The journey will not be easy, and we will stumble along the way. But we will persevere, knowing that we have each other and that we will eventually prevail. Civil rights activists in the United States in the 1960s, freedom fighters in India during the first half of the 20th century, and slave revolts in Haiti have taught us that many different paths can take one to social justice, but none of them were achieved without struggle and persistence.

Paulo Freire (1970), a Brazilian philosopher and educator whose work on critical pedagogy remains one of the most significant contributions in the area of education and social justice, discusses the importance of developing a consciousness and awareness of social injustice. It is hard to challenge it if we don't see it or acknowledge it. Consciousness raising has been a strategy that women's groups have used for a long time. Sharing our truths with each other and listening and acknowledging those parts of each other's lives that have long been denied or dismissed is a critical step toward social justice. In the words of Audre Lorde, American writer and activist (1984), self-described "black, lesbian, mother, warrior, poet":

> We can learn to work and speak when we are afraid in the same way we have learned to work and speak when we are tired. For we have been socialized to respect fear more than our own needs for language and definition, and while we wait in silence for that final luxury of fearlessness, the weight of that silence will choke us. The fact that we are here and that I

> speak these words is an attempt to break that silence and bridge some of those differences between us, for it is not difference which immobilizes us, but silence. And there are so many silences to be broken.

As women we are taught to be "well-behaved," which often means not questioning the status quo. As a result, our desire for approval and for maintaining the facade of civility keeps us silent and complicit in our own oppression. Shedding light on these tools of oppression and making them visible is part of the process of developing consciousness and awareness of social injustice.

The next step is to analyze and make visible hidden power hierarchies by asking questions such as the following: Who benefits and who pays for a proposed change? Who is at the table and who is missing when decisions are being made? How are those with the least power affected by proposed changes? We also need to deconstruct binaries based on race, gender, and other social identities and refuse to accept that socially constructed categories and power differentials are somehow natural and inevitable and cannot be changed. Let us disrupt the dominant narrative by creating what-if scenarios as counter narratives. Men and women are not dichotomous categories, and the recent work of our nonbinary colleagues (Turner, 2000) has taught us much about gender fluidity and the need to create space for a continuum rather than a binary. But most importantly we need to always follow the lead of the oppressed. Women, especially those of us who are the most disadvantaged, need to set the agenda and define and name the issues that need to be addressed. The rest of us can hold the space where their silences can be broken and coalesce around these issues, looking for convergence of interests, building coalitions, and seeking global connections whenever possible (Mohanty, 2003).

What Is Compassion?

According to Karen Armstrong (2011), British author and commentator on comparative religions, compassion is defined and practiced by many different religious traditions, but what they all share in common could be distilled down to the *golden rule*—treat others the way you want to be treated. According to Jack Kornfield, American mindfulness practitioner and teacher, compassion is what happens when love meets distress or suffering. **Compassion is defined within the field of positive psychology as an emotional response to the suffering of others accompanied by a genuine desire to alleviate the suffering without expectation of reciprocity or reward.** According to Geshe Thupten Jinpa, Tibetan Buddhist monk, principal author of compassion cultivation training offered at Stanford University and English translator for the Dalai Lama since 1985, compassion as an emotional response has a cognitive aspect, an affective aspect, and a motivational aspect. The cognitive aspect is saying that I understand your suffering. The affective aspect is saying that I feel your suffering, and the motivational aspect is saying that I want to alleviate your suffering.

Invitation to reflect: Take a moment to bring to mind someone that you know is in distress and try to put yourself in their shoes. Imagine for a moment what they might need to help alleviate their suffering.

Research has shown that compassion is a natural human response that has played a key role in our very survival (Seppala, 2013). The idea of "survival of the fittest" is often incorrectly attributed to Charles Darwin and used as the basis for Social Darwinism by English biologist and sociologist Spencer (1864), Galton, and others. But, in fact, Darwin suggested that kindness and compassion is more critical for survival than competition. During the pandemic there were many instances of compassionate behavior. One showed in the story of the young boy who went to his local hospital every day at the time of a nursing staff shift change to stand outside and play his violin for workers and remind them that someone cares. We have also heard of acts of intolerance and fear where medical professionals have been harassed at grocery stores and other public spaces. According to the most recent World Happiness Report (Helliwell, et al., 2022), benevolence has increased since the pandemic, as compared to pre-pandemic levels, by 8% if measured as a percent of the total population and by 25% in the 2017–2019 frequency of benevolent acts across all regions of the world. Benevolence includes helping strangers, donating, and volunteering and is probably underestimated because it does not cover all the unseen, unreported acts of kindness.

Research studies have also shown that leading a compassionate life with strong and meaningful social connections is related to greater physical and mental well-being (Diener & Seligman, 2002). We are happier when we are more compassionate. Dunn (2008), Canadian social psychologist, found that giving to others gives human beings more pleasure than receiving from others. American social scientists Fowler and Christakis (2010) have found that kindness is contagious, and its impact is sustained over time. One act of kindness begets more acts of kindnesses, creating an ever-widening ripple effect. While compassion is a natural response, research (Leiberg et al., 2011) has shown that compassion cultivation training can help enhance our capacity for compassion.

It is important to distinguish compassion from other similar concepts such as empathy, sympathy, and pity, which are all reactions to the plight of others. "Empathy" refers to our capacity as human beings to recognize and feel someone else's emotions. Empathy requires being able to put ourselves in someone else's situation and feel what they are feeling but it does not include wanting to alleviate that suffering. As a result, empathy can lead to burnout and fatigue and often leads to more suffering and despair. Social neuroscience research (Singer & Klimecki, 2014) has shown us that empathy and compassion responses involve different parts of the brain and follow different neural pathways such that empathy elicits negative affect whereas compassion elicits positive affect. "Compassion" leads to positive affect because it allows us to find our common humanity with those in distress, but instead of creating a sense of helplessness it leads to clarity and action. "Sympathy," on the other hand, is a feeling of care or concern for someone else's suffering without actually experiencing that suffering. "Pity" is the near enemy of compassion in that there is a discomfort at the suffering of others, but it is accompanied with a sense of superiority. Pity might motivate you to "save" or "rescue" someone because you see them as less than and unable to help themselves, whereas compassion motivates you to support someone in distress because you see your common humanity and interconnectedness and are stronger together. In the words of Lilla Watson, Aboriginal educator and activist, "If you have come to help me, then you are wasting your time. But if you have come because your liberation is tied up with mine, then let us work together." In short, empathy is the emotional experience of another person's feelings (I feel your suffering), while sympathy is a feeling of care or concern for someone else (I care about your suffering), and pity is a feeling of discomfort at someone else's distress and is usually accompanied with a feeling of superiority (I feel sorry for you).

It is often easy to feel compassion for those who look like us or someone with whom we are able to connect with at some level or someone we think "deserves" our compassion. It is a lot harder to extend compassion unconditionally and unequivocally to those who don't look like us or we deem as less worthy, and that is where our socially conditioned biases and prejudices start showing up. In a research study (Avenanti et al., 2010), a team of Italian scientists showed people a video with a hand in pain. Typically, when humans see someone else in pain it produces a physiological response. The participants in the study were shown a white hand, a black hand, and a "blue alien" hand. White participants produced the most response to the white hand, then the alien hand, and then the black hand. Black participants produced the most response to the black hand, then the alien hand, and then the white hand. Research has shown that we have to train and practice extending kindness and compassion to all sentient beings to combat the effects of social conditioning.

The idea of deeming someone worthy of our compassion might also come from the lauding and rewarding of *individualism* as the dominant paradigm in the world today. If we believe that only individual effort should be rewarded and what we have accomplished is a result of individual effort, then someone's negative outcome or distress might be seen as resulting from their lack of effort and therefore, not worthy of compassion. But if we believe that we are all interdependent and that everything we achieve is based on collective/community efforts, then compassion might be an easier response. The fact is that as human beings none of us would have survived to adulthood if someone hadn't taken care of us as babies. Throughout our lives we rely on each other for survival, social connection, sharing of ideas, care when we are vulnerable, and validation when we are strong. Compassion requires that we celebrate our interdependence instead of fearing it. Our fear of scarcity and not having enough and believing that we have to each look out for ourselves because no one else will might also make it harder for us to be compassionate. Finally, greed and the push to accumulate more and more material resources as a standard of success is another major deterrent to compassion. The earth provides generously for all of us without condition or judgment. A tree provides shade to all who need it without first checking whether we deserve it. And yet as human beings we have been led to believe that we own the earth or parts of it, and therefore we get to decide who gets to have shelter, who gets to have food, who gets to thrive and survive. These are some of the key questions that we must grapple with as we face a global pandemic, climate change, and increasing inequality.

Compassion and social justice are intimately tied together, and each is necessary for the other to exist. Reading this book and others like it might lead to anger, frustration, and even helplessness at the enormity of the social injustice that we are facing. While anger, frustration, and despair are natural reactions to social injustice and can even inspire us to action, the actions themselves need to come out of love. We need to save the world not because we are angry or guilty or fearful but because we love it and we belong to it and each other. In the words of Martin Luther King Jr., "I can never be what I ought to be until you are what you ought to be. You can never be what you ought to be until I am what I ought to be." We are here to embrace our membership in each other's lives, to discover our interconnectedness, invest in each other's well-being and to always remember that we belong. Recognizing and celebrating our interdependence is the key to social justice. If the pandemic has taught us just one lesson it has to be that none of us are going to make it on our own. We are not alone. We are in this together.

Invitation to reflect: Take a moment to reflect on acts of compassion that you have observed or have engaged in and how it made you feel.

Key Takeaways

Below are the key ideas to take away from this chapter:

- Social justice requires that all people have the same rights and are treated fairly such that it leads to equitable opportunities and equitable outcomes for all. There is no country in the world that treats women as well as it treats men. Therefore, gender inequality is a social justice issue.
- The global gender gap index is a measure that combines four dimensions—economic participation, political participation, educational attainment, and health and survival—to give us an overall measure of gender equality across 156 countries.
- The unprecedented upheaval in our economic and social structures over the last 18 months has had a devastating effect on gender equality, but it has also provided us with an opportunity to envision a different path forward that addresses the triple crises of job loss, climate change, and a fractured care economy.
- Social injustice is initiated and perpetuated by systems of oppression and exploitation. An oppressive structure systematically confers rights and privileges on the dominant group, which benefits from and has power over the subordinate group. Members of the subordinate group are systemically denied the autonomy and capacity to thrive, and their contributions are marginalized and appropriated by the dominant group.
- "Compassion" is defined within the field of positive psychology as an emotional response to the suffering of others, accompanied by a genuine desire to alleviate the suffering without expectation of reciprocity or reward.
- Compassion and social justice are intimately tied together, and each is necessary for the other to exist. We need to save the world not because we are angry or guilty or fearful but because we love it and we belong to it and each other.

Comprehension Questions

Directions: Use what you have learned in this chapter to help you respond to the questions below:

- Why have women been disproportionately affected by the pandemic?
- Use different aspects of the concept of social justice to explain in your own words why gender inequality is a social justice issue.
- According to Adams and Bell, oppression is restrictive, pervasive, cumulative, based on socially constructed categories, hierarchical, hegemonic, internalized, intersectional and has consequences for all. Identify and discuss any two of these features within the context of the Global Gender Gap

index.

- Explain how the concept of compassion is different from the concepts of empathy and pity. Why do acts of compassion lead to greater well-being?
- How are compassion and social justice linked? Why do we need compassion to create a more just and equitable world?

References

Adams, M. & Bell, L. (2016). *Teaching for diversity and social justice* (3rd ed.). Routledge.

Armstrong, K. (2011). Twelve steps to a compassionate life. Anchor Publishers.

Avenanti, A., Sirigu, A. & Aglioti, S. (2010). Racial bias reduces empathic sensorimotor resonance with other-race pain. *Current Biology,* 20(11), 1018–1022,

Crenshaw, K. (1991). Mapping the Margins: Intersectionality, identity politics and violence against women of color. *Stanford Law Review,* 43(6), 1241–1299.

Diener, E., Seligman, M. E. P. (2002). Very happy people. *Psychological Science,* 13(1), 81–84.

Dunn, E., Aknin, L. B., & Norton, M. I. (2008). Spending money on others promotes happiness. *Science, 319,* 1687–1688.

Fowler, J. & Christakis, N. (2010). Cooperative behavior cascades in human social networks. *Proceedings of the National Academy of Sciences,* 107 (12) 5334–5338.

Freire, P. (1970). *Pedagogy of the oppressed.* New York: Seabury.

Global Gender Gap Report 2021. World Economic Forum.

Helliwell, J. F., Layard, R., Sachs, J. D., De Neve, J.-E., Aknin, L. B., & Wang, S. (Eds.). (2022). *World Happiness Report 2022.* New York: Sustainable Development Solutions Network.

International Labour Organization (ILO). (2021). *World Social Protection Report 2020–2022: Social Protection at the Crossroads—Making a Decisive Turn for a Better Future.* Geneva: ILO.

Leiberg, S., Klimecki, O., & Singer, T. (2011). Short-term compassion training increases prosocial behavior in a newly developed prosocial game. *PLoS ONE* 6(3): e17798.

Lorde, A. (1984). *Sister outsider.* Trumansburg, NY: Crossing Press.

Mohanty, C. T. (2003). *Feminism without borders: Decolonizing theory, practicing solidarity.* Durham, NC: Duke University Press.

Rawls, J. (1971). *A theory of justice.* Belknap Press.

Rawls, J. (2001). *Justice as fairness: A restatement.* Belknap Press.

Sen, A. (2010). *The idea of justice.* Penguin, UK.

Seppala, E. (2013, May/June). The compassionate mind. *Observer.* Association for Psychological Sciences. https://www.psychologicalscience.org/observer/the-compassionate-mind

Singer, T. & Klimecki, O. (2014). Empathy and compassion. *Current Biology,* 24(18), R875-R878.

Spencer, H. (1864). *Principles of biology.* London.

Turner, W. (2000). *A genealogy of queer theory.* Philadelphia: Temple University Press.

UN Women. (2021). *Beyond Covid-19: A feminist plan for sustainability and social justice.* Research and Data Section, UN Women.

Chapter 2

Concepts of Economic Development

> Development is much more than increases in GDP and the growth of markets; it's about the fulfillment of human potential in all its dimensions—for each and every one. It's about economic as well as political democracy.
>
> —Lourdes Beneria, Spanish American economist (2003: 167–68)

From Local Stories to Global Visions

In 2007, the Achuar community, a group of indigenous peoples from the Amazon rainforests of Ecuador and Peru, took a stand against oil companies that wanted to encroach on their lands The community have been stewards of their ancestral lands for thousands of years. Their ancestral wisdom is based on principles of self-sufficiency and self-determination and increasingly the need to protect themselves and their lands from encroachment. The Ecuadorian government started granting oil concessions in the early part of the 20th century and the irreparable damage to the earth and to the peoples of this land started to mount. I heard about them when their lawsuit made history as one of the first times that indigenous communities were able to receive compensation for the untold loss they suffered at the hands of oil companies. They also recognized the need to work in partnership with people outside of their community to protect the rainforests and to remind us that the survival of all beings crucially depends on the rainforests. We have much to learn from the Achuar people about taking only what we need and living in harmony with our natural environment, which provides us with everything we need to sustain ourselves and flourish.

Invitation to reflect: Take a moment to reflect on what our lives might be like if we consumed only what we needed.

Introduction

Chapter 1 provides a shared understanding of the concepts of social justice, oppression, and compassion. In chapter 2 we will focus our attention on the concept of development from social justice perspectives. There is no one universal concept of development. It changes across time, across disciplines, across schools of thought, and across nations. The term "development" implies some notion of change and can therefore only be understood in a historical context. Often an attempt is made to argue that development is a technical matter and is divorced from ideology and morality. In truth, adopting a particular definition of development sets a specific agenda, bringing along with it the values and assumptions of that conceptualization. Therefore, there is a need to bring issues of ethical choice out into the open so that they can be discussed. If one is willing to do that, then one must also be willing to face that what is moral or ethical in different cultures may differ. In addition, value systems themselves are constantly changing from within and from the outside.

Most definitions of "development" rely heavily on Western European thought and experience, ranging from the emphasis on technological change to industrialization. During most of the early conceptualization of development and even today the ideal society is assumed to look very much like the United States. European colonialism has also affected the nature of the development process, not only by conditioning the history of many nations but by leaving behind institutions that continue to influence development in these countries. The creation of international agencies that are staffed by Western-born (or at least Western-trained) personnel further influences the development path taken by these countries. In addition, because of the widespread availability of the internet and other communication technologies there is a demonstration effect putting pressure on low-income countries to hurry up and develop. In this chapter, we ask how and when the concept of development was socially and politically constructed. We go back in history to explore the context within which this particular conceptualization of development became the hegemonic view. We examine alternative conceptualizations of development and consider the policy implications of adopting different concepts of development.

Economic Growth Approach to Development

Colombian-born American anthropologist, Arturo Escobar (1995), argues that starting with the Truman Doctrine, the concept of development was socially constructed by using the economic model that originated in the United States and in Western Europe as the gold standard to which all countries must aspire regardless of their specific historical, social, cultural, and economic conditions. In his inaugural address in 1949, American President Harry Truman decreed with one speech that more than half of the world's population was "underdeveloped" and that their lives were miserable and primitive. Truman believed that science, technology, and greater production was the key to achieving a better life of material prosperity. He assumed that the rest of the world must want the American life, completely ignoring the fact that, not only were there many people in the United States who were denied this life, but that people in different parts of the world might not aspire toward the *American Dream*. Over time this view of the world became legitimized as the only way of looking at the world, and other worldviews were effectively silenced or marginalized. Since post-WWI, this discourse of development became the dominant paradigm. Additionally, the notion of the "Third World" was created and indelibly imprinted on our collective imagination through regimes of representation.

Invitation to reflect: Take a moment to reflect on the images that come to your mind when you think about the "Third World." Reflect on when and how these associations were first formed.

The end of the Second World War brought with it the ascendancy of the United States. This was challenged by the rising power of the former Soviet Union, socialist regimes in Eastern Europe, and communist China, leading to the notions of three worlds: the free industrialized nations of the First World, the communist industrialized nations of the Second World, and the poor, non-industrialized nations of the Third World. "Poverty," defined as those living below a certain per capita income, became the criteria by which countries were ranked and valued. Poverty became problematized, and poor countries became the subject of intense intervention by rich industrialized countries. Poverty was seen largely as a technical problem that needed to be solved with science and technology and efficient use of resources. Escobar argues that this positioning of the United States and Western Europe as 'developed' countries and all other countries as "underdeveloped" countries implied a power relationship whereby the "developed" countries are the knowers (the adults) and the rest of the world is ignorant, backward (the infant) and needs to be helped and shown the way. Countries started seeing themselves as being "underdeveloped" and how to become developed became their central problem to solve. The dominant, hegemonic worldview focused on rapid economic growth accompanied by industrialization and urbanization as the path to development. This view ignored the historical reality that the *American Dream* was founded on enslavement of Africans and extermination of Native peoples of this land. **Economic growth is defined as the process by which real per capita income of a country increases over a long period of time. It implies a qualitative change in the economy via improved performance of the factors of production and improved techniques of production. This could be achieved by capital accumulation and the use of science and technology.**

The period between 1920 and 1960 was marked by a process of decolonization in Africa and Asia and a changing neocolonial relationship between European colonial powers and nascent nation states in Africa and Asia. Although most Latin American countries achieved political independence in the 19th century, many of these countries were also subject to the same kinds of policy interventions. The World Bank mission to Colombia in 1949 was one of the first manifestations of this approach. While there was much debate among academics and policymakers during the 1970s in Latin America, Africa, and Asia about the kinds of policies that might lead to development, the need for development itself was never questioned. It was only in the 1980s and 1990s that authors such as Said (1979), Mudimbe (1988), Mohanty (1991), and others started questioning the colonization of the development discourse and the way that different parts of Africa and Asia were depicted and acted upon in the name of development.

Motivation Behind Truman Doctrine

It is possible that some policymakers genuinely wanted to "help underdeveloped" countries and believed that the US model was the best one and could and should work for everyone. Perhaps they were moved by what they perceived to be the misery of the people in Third World countries and wanted to alleviate their misery. But this is where compassion gives way to pity. Firstly, if our desire to help people is based on our assumed superiority, then the solutions we think are going to help might make the situation worse. By contrast, if the desire to help is seen as an interaction between equals, then the impact might be more effective. For example, the reconstruction of Europe was seen as a major priority for the United States. Between 1945 and 1950 the United States provided more than $19 billion in foreign assistance to Western Europe as part of the Marshall Plan, which allowed Europe to rebuild their economies more or less on their own terms. Whereas the United States provided less than $150 million to all Third World countries combined and several attached conditions left many of these countries worse off.

Secondly, a model that works in one country within a particular social, historical, cultural context might not work in another country with a different social, historical, cultural context. There was a naïve and arrogant faith in the power of western science and technology to solve the problem of development, which effectively privileged certain ways of knowing and marginalized other forms of knowledge and other forms of technology. According to this conceptualization, development must include a move from "the traditional to the modern," implying an increased control over one's environment via scientific knowledge and rational thought and action. The poor were seen as incapable of defining and solving their own problems. They were seen as helpless, backward, and ignorant, and in need of intervention from people and institutions millions of miles away who somehow knew what they needed and how they should and could be helped.

I am reminded of a story of a group of World Bank experts that went to a village in rural India. They observed the women of the village walking to a river a couple of miles away to fetch water every morning. They wanted to *help* these women and decided to install a water pump in the village so that they would not have to walk to the river. They came back a year later and found that no one was using the pump. They asked one of the women why they weren't using the pump, and she said that the time the women spent walking to the river was their time to chat with each other and share their joys and tribulations. They enjoyed that time together. Had they been asked what they needed they might have suggested a school for their children or medical supplies or other more pressing needs rather than a water pump. The water pump itself is not the problem. It is entirely possible that in those in another village might well have wanted a water pump. Asking the people you are trying to help how they might want to be helped is the critical missing step in this story.

Finally, not every society has the same values, dreams, and aspirations as that of the United States. As we saw with the Achuar community and other indigenous peoples throughout the Americas, living in harmony with the rainforest and taking only what they needed was more important than rapid economic growth and industrialization. They did not want the kind of development that was being imposed on them without consultation or permission.

Invitation to reflect: Take a moment to imagine countries/communities being ranked and ordered by another criterion (for example, number of songs that the citizens can sing; number of new trees planted; number of acts of kindness). Which criteria would you choose? How would it make you feel if the criteria were chosen by another country and imposed on you, leaving you had no say in choosing the criteria?

The Truman doctrine was also motivated by the consolidation of US power over the world capitalist system, which required unfettered access to new markets for US products and cheap sources of raw materials. The establishment of the Bretton Woods institutions of the International Monetary Fund (IMF) and the World Bank played a critical role in shaping and managing development policy. Development became synonymous with economic growth and the main ingredient in economic growth was considered to be capital accumulation. Since most newly independent Third World countries did not have capital, they immediately became reliant on First World countries and their accompanying institutions for access to capital. These loans were often given in exchange for privileged access to raw materials or commitments to buy products from the lender nations. The unequal power relationship between First and Third World countries led to unequal exchange, which often further impoverished Third World countries. For example, several countries in Latin America got into a spiraling debt crisis where they were taking loans to repay loans. In other cases, borrowing countries were expected to change their crop production patterns from food to cash crop production, which led to large scale famine.

Indian born political scientist Shirin Rai (2011) further argues that the Cold War and the post-colonial reconstruction of much of the world during the second half of the 20th century framed the discussion about development. The battle for political and cultural influence between the United States and the former Soviet Union was fought largely in the Third World. Most of the 150 wars fought in the second half of the 20th century were waged in Third World countries with direct or indirect participation of the two superpowers. Warding off communism became one of the most important underpinnings of the development discourse and development aid, which was often tied to specific military and political agendas.

A blend of arrogance and benevolence that many development planners share denies people cognitive respect of their own perception of reality, which is theirs as a basic right. If there is any universal aspiration, it must be for every person to want to be treated by others as a being of worth regardless of his/her utility to others. All people and societies should be given that cognitive respect. Quoting from Sartre's play Dirty Hands in which Hugo asks, *"What is the use of struggling for the liberation of men if we despise them to the point of brainwashing them?"*

On the other hand, one might also ask is there no common ground? Is there no international morality that we can agree upon as human beings? If societies in distress are faced with the cruel choice between bread and dignity, these questions will remain with us. Perhaps the real challenge of development is to seek solutions that accept neither hunger nor the terror of indignity.

Well-Being Approach to Development

Standard economic theory is based on the idea that economic growth translates to more goods and services, which translates to higher utility and higher well-being. Classical economists like Adam Smith recognized that human happiness or well-being is only partially based on material wealth. But these nonpecuniary factors are much more difficult to define and quantify. In addition, the work of these 18th-century economists was influenced by the huge increases in physical output and pursuit of wealth that was ushered in by the dawn of the industrial revolution.

Until the second half of the 20th century, well-being and happiness was mostly the domain of philosophers. While there are many different definitions of well-being, economics as a discipline primarily adopted the principle of utility given by English philosopher Jeremy Bentham wherein happiness is associated with pleasure and absence of pain. Any object that provides benefits, increases pleasure, or decreases pain promotes happiness. Bentham identifies happiness as a unitary sensation and largely ignores the problem of interpersonal comparisons and the problem of evil pleasures. He also ignores the fact that activities can have an intrinsic pleasure and are not always means to an end. By contrast, Greek philosopher Aristotle's concept of eudaimonia identifies happiness as flourishing human living, a kind of living that is inclusive of all that has intrinsic value—ethical, intellectual, political, love, and friendship. Pleasure is not identical with happiness, but it usually accompanies many of the activities associated with happiness. According to this conceptualization, happiness must have the following characteristics:

- It must be final—inclusive of all that has intrinsic value.
- It must be self-sufficient—you should not need anything else to qualify it.
- It must be active—being in a coma might mean no pain but it cannot mean happiness.
- It must be generally available—everyone can be happy.
- It must be relatively stable—more than a fleeting experience.
- It is not the mere aggregation of its parts—it is the way it is all put together.
- It is activity in accordance with excellence—involves striving even if that striving involves short-term pain.
- It is living a good life—there is a normative element to it.

English philosopher John Stuart Mill combines elements of Bentham and Aristotle. He still focused on pleasure, but he questioned that it is unitary. He also questioned the notion that all kinds of pleasure bring happiness. He allowed for the intrinsic value of activities that bring a sense of dignity. But Mill disagreed with Aristotle that courage in the face of adversity makes one happy. He argued that adversity makes one unhappy even if one has the courage to deal with it.

Easterlin Paradox and a Theory of Well-Being

There has been mounting empirical evidence demonstrating that economic growth does not always lead to greater well-being. These studies have challenged one of the most basic assumptions of economics as a discipline. One of the earliest studies (Easterlin, 1974) that challenged this idea is called the Easterlin paradox. American economist Richard Easterlin used data from many different countries and found that within a country, at a given moment in time, well-being and income are correlated. But as incomes rise over time, well-being remains fairly constant. He also found that the correlation between income and well-being is weak across countries at a given moment in time. A more recent study (Diener & Seligman, 2004) found that even though GDP has tripled over the past 50 years in the United States, life satisfaction has remained constant, recognizing that short-run fluctuations in income and happiness are correlated but long-term trends are not.

Several explanations are proffered for the Easterlin paradox. One of them is called *set point theory*, which assumes that each person has a set point of happiness based on personality and genetics. Objective life events may temporarily deflect a person from their set point, but in time hedonic adaptation will return the person to their set point (Brickman & Campbell, 1971). The question is not whether there is adaptation but whether the adaptation is complete. Studies have shown that adaptation to changes in some circumstances is more complete than in others (Lucas et al., 2003). For example, adaptation to changes in health and changes in marital status is less complete whereas adaptation to changes in income is more complete. Other studies have found that intentional acts of kindness and altruism can have a stronger impact on happiness than changes in circumstances (Sheldon & Lyubomirsky, 2006).

Invitation to reflect: Take a moment to reflect on what happiness means to you. How is it different from well-being?

Easterlin (2005) took the findings of these studies to build a better theory of well-being which posits that a person's well-being depends on a variety of monetary and nonmonetary factors, such as one's health, family and social relationships, job, etc. Each person will have aspirations about each of these domains and current attainment in each domain. Well-being depends upon the gap between aspirations and attainment in each domain and the relative importance of each domain. But aspirations are not fixed. Habit formation affects aspirations because your aspirations change based on your own consumption, i.e., a hedonic treadmill. Interdependent preferences tell us that our aspirations are also based on what everyone else has or does not have—a social treadmill. However, Easterlin found that these two treadmills do not operate the same way across domains. Both these treadmills are less complete in health and family than with material goods. Therefore, Easterlin argues that people should allocate more effort to those domains where adaptation is less than complete than those domains where adaptation is more complete, and policy should also follow that same path. In other words, policies that focus on economic growth alone will not lead to improvements in well-being. We also need to focus on policies that give us the opportunity to improve other domains that are important for our well-being, such as our health and our relationships. Recent discussions about work–life balance might be explained by this theory.

Anthropological Foundations of Economic Man

Another reason why economic theory is unable to address happiness in any meaningful way stems from the anthropological basis for human behavior within economics, i.e., individualism. The *Economic Man* is assumed to be atomistic, isolated from any other human being, asocial, whose true nature lies outside of human relationality and who maximizes utility. If the definition of self-interest is broad enough and we expand the contents of the utility function enough, we can explain pretty much any kind of behavior, which implies that economic behavior does not have to be characterized by selfish actions. Therefore, the problem is not the assumption of self-interested behavior but the assumption of *non-tuism*—carrying out economic transactions without caring about the identity of the person you are exchanging with. Non-tuism is the negation of relationality. We need to accept that there is a difference between the relationship between individual and object and relationship between persons. Italian economist Stefano Zamagni (2006) urges economists to replace the individual with person who exists in relation to others. This would imply a change from the individual to the relational paradigm.

The relational paradigm relies on being able to see the interests of others while distancing yourself from your own interest. It also relies on empathy, which means that you are able to see the other person's perspective. *At its core, relationality is not only accepting the right of others to exist but the necessity of others to exist so that I can exist in relation to him/her.* If we assume that sociality is reciprocal recognition between people, that we need each other, then the need for social interaction is a need in and of itself. In fact, individual needs can only be understood once we have established each person in relation to everyone else. Kahneman's moment-based measure of subjective well-being provides evidence that there is a clear association between positive affect and social interaction and that this association is not necessarily only derived from deep relationships. English economist Robert Sugden (2006) argues that we derive happiness from social interaction because of our need for correspondence of sentiments. Our experiences and emotions need to be affirmed, shared, and acknowledged by other human beings for them to become meaningful and significant. Perhaps that might explain the popularity of social media in recent years.

Well-Being as Human Flourishing

According to American psychologist Martin Seligman (2011), **well–being is defined as multifaceted human flourishing. These facets include positive affect, engagement, relationships and social support, meaning and purpose, and accomplishment and autonomy** (PERMA):

- "Positive affect" refers to the experience of positive emotions, which has been shown to increase well-being and life chances (Lyubomirsky et al., 2005).
- "Engagement" refers to the state of being focused on and completely in sync with a particular task or activity. Engagement requires that the tasks we are involved in are challenging enough to be interesting, but not so challenging that they are frustrating.
- Social support that protects, respects, values, and nurtures people has been recognized as one of the most important determinants of well-being (Reis & Gable, 2003).
- "Meaning and purpose" is defined as *"feeling of belonging and serving something larger than the self"* (Seligman, 2011). As human beings we need to find purpose to be truly happy.
- "Accomplishment" refers to the feeling of achievement or competence and is closely related to the psychological needs for autonomy and efficacy identified by Deci and Ryan's (2000) self-determination theory.

The well-being approach lies at the intersection of the disciplines of psychology, economics, and philosophy and has expanded the dimensionality of the economic development discourse. Recent developments in the measurement of well-being have created the opportunity for research and evidence-based policies with a greater potential for improving our overall well-being.

Capabilities Approach to Development

Nobel laureate Amartya Sen (1999) argues that the narrow definition of development as economic growth fails to consider that economic growth may be "a means to an end, but it is not an end in and of itself." Sen argues that having the freedom to live in ways we value is the end goal of development. Sen defines **development as an expansion of entitlements and the capabilities that these entitlements generate to live in ways that we value.** These include the freedom to fully participate in the economic, social, and political life of the community to which one belongs. For example, according to Sen, when large groups of people are denied economic opportunities such as safe working conditions or fair wages or experience social deprivation such as lack of access to education or the right to love and marry someone of their choice, these are *unfreedoms*. The task of development is to remove the chief causes of *unfreedoms,* namely poverty, tyranny, repressive regimes, intolerance, and lack of universal social support systems.

Invitation to reflect: Take a moment to reflect on some freedoms and unfreedoms that you experience. Are they related to your income level alone or are there other factors?

"Entitlements" refers to the set of alternative bundles of all that we value that a person can command in a society using the totality of rights and opportunities that she or he has. For example, in a pure market economy if a person has only her labor power to sell and she is able to get a wage of $200, then her entitlements refer to the set of all bundles costing no more than $200 that she can buy, and the limit is set by the ownership (endowment) or exchange possibilities. On the basis of these entitlements, she can acquire some capabilities, i.e., the ability to be nourished, the ability to be educated, etc., and fail to acquire others. It also includes the notion of being able to choose among alternatives. In other words, the larger the set of capabilities that a person's entitlements generate, the more developed the country will be according to this definition. Even if the person chooses not to acquire some of these capabilities, the very fact that the person could is important.

For example, there is a difference between one who chooses to fast due to a religious or health related reason and one who is starving because they do not have access to food. Most people only have their labor to sell, in which case their entitlements crucially depend upon their ability to get a job, the wages they receive, the prices of goods, etc. The problem of starvation, hunger, and famine can then be seen as a problem of entitlements, rather than a problem of population growth or food supply. Entitlements may also operate through social security or what families can get from the state. Entitlements are partially determined by incomes, but not completely. For example, an increase in income does not give the person the ability to be educated if there are no schools in the village he lives in. In the extreme, the entitlement to live in a malaria-free environment is not a matter of personal income.

Some might argue that at a macro level, economic growth increases the ability of the state to provide social support services for all. However, empirical evidence has shown us that there might not always be the political willingness to provide social support. For example, in 2019 GDP per capita in current dollars in the United States was $65,144 and the adult male mortality rate per 1000 males was 137.5. By comparison, the GDP per capita in current dollars in China was only $10,216 but the adult male mortality rate per 1000 males was 93.7. In another example, the GDP per capita in current dollars in Costa Rica was $12,669 and the life expectancy at birth was 80.3 years, compared to the United States where life expectancy at birth was 78.8 years. The relationship between income and life expectancy is based primarily on state expenditure on health care and the income of the poor. It is also based on access to health care. If different segments of society have differential access to healthcare, then this could lead to different life expectancies. For example, mean income in current dollars for African American males in 2019 was $45,423 with a life expectancy at birth of 72.2 years, compared to Costa Rica, which had a GDP per capita in current dollars of $12,669 in 2019 with a male life expectancy of 77.7 years. Countries like Costa Rica and Sri Lanka have taught us that a country does not have to wait for high economic growth to provide social support services for all.

According to Sen (1999), *"capabilities can be expanded by public expenditures and public policy and public policy can be enhanced by capabilities."* One of the primary freedoms for a society is to be able to decide for itself the life they value and want to live. In that sense, development as an expansion of freedoms is both the primary end and the primary means to that end. Sen emphasizes the importance of process and outcome. One cannot achieve an expansion in freedoms through a process that involves a curtailment of freedoms. We have seen examples of countries that have curtailed right to due process during times of crisis. Different kinds of freedoms are also interrelated such that an expansion in one kind of freedom can lead to an expansion of another kind of freedom. This view of development sees human beings as active participants and agents of change versus passive recipients of development.

Feminist Approach to Development

Feminist economists have coalesced around a definition that **sees development as a process that provides for the survival, sustenance, and flourishing of life** (Nelson and Power, 2018). Through a process of dialogue and collaboration over the last 20 to 30 years, feminist economists have adopted six core assumptions or *"methodological starting points"* (Power, 2004). Let's examine individually each core assumption.

First, the care economy is a central and essential part of any economic system (Ferber & Nelson, 1993; Folbre, 1994). The COVID pandemic has highlighted the inequitable way in which the economy relies on the unpaid labor of mostly women in the care economy. By explicitly making this assumption, feminist economists acknowledge and recognize the interdependent and interconnected nature of care work. They challenge the dominant conceptualization of development, which often renders the workers that provide care work—mostly women—invisible. The dominant economic model based on economic growth clearly separated the economic sphere from the other spheres. According to the economic growth approach, the economic sphere is the privileged sphere in which "productive activity" occurs, and if a country wants to achieve rapid economic growth it needs to promote activities in this sphere. The private sphere of the household and the family was rendered invisible and considered "unproductive" and therefore not worthy of attention. Different theories of development were articulated regarding how rapid economic growth in the economic sphere could be achieved. These theories led to different policies and strategies of development, which were promoted by the United States and Western Europe and organizations such as the World Bank and the International Monetary Fund. Although they might have worked in some cases, most of the time these policies ignored the private sphere of the household where much of the care work occurred. The feminist definition of development places the care economy in the center of the analysis.

Second, similar to the care economy, the global economy relies on the exploitation of the environment, assuming that these resources are costless and limitless. The impact of overexploitation and overconsumption of natural resources falls disproportionately on marginalized groups, especially women living in low-income countries who contribute least to overconsumption. Women—especially those in rural areas who are usually responsible for providing food and water for their families—find it harder to forage for food and water because of deforestation. Women and children are also harder hit by pollution caused by unclean cooking and heating fuel. In addition, women have unequal access to natural resources, especially land. The feminist definition of development recognizes that we need to be better stewards of our natural resources and make choices that prioritize the well-being of future generations and the long-term sustainability of our practices. This approach suggests that the problem is not underdevelopment as defined by the economic growth approach, but rather overdevelopment and the accompanying overconsumption that it promotes.

Third, economic success in terms of outcomes is measured not by real GDP per capita but the well-being of all people, especially those who are the most marginalized in society. "Well-being" is a much broader concept than economic growth and brings attention to the composition and distribution of resources. It also identifies productive work as that which creates the conditions for all people to survive, thrive and flourish (Floro, 1995).

Fourth, economic success is measured in terms of processes that encourage greater and more equitable participation by all people in all aspects of economic, political, and social life (Sen, 1999).

Fifth, ethical judgments are an inevitable and desired part of economic development (Beneria, 2003; Nussbaum, 2003). The economic growth approach claims to be ahistorical and apolitical while eschewing ethical considerations. The feminist approach suggests that all approaches rely on underlying ethical judgments and prefers that we make these judgments explicit and transparent.

Sixth, the feminist approach embraces intersectionality regarding race, class, sexual orientation, and other social identities, which challenges the homogeneity of women's experiences and allows for a richer and more inclusive understanding of women's experiences across space and time. These six core assumptions work together to define economic development as a process of *social provisioning*. The feminist plan for post-COVID recovery announced by UN Women in September 2021 asserts

> ... this new economic paradigm would ensure sustainable livelihoods for all and would stop treating unpaid care work and the environment as limitless resources that can be used for free and depleted without cost or consequence. Instead, it would put economic policies at the service of sustainability, gender equality, and social justice. (UN Women, 2021, p. 12)

This plan calls for transformative change by focusing on the synergies between sustainability and gender justice and putting care for all people and care for the planet front and center: Creating decent jobs in green sectors and in the care economy; supporting sustainable agricultural practices to create food security for all, and treating the care economy as a public good that needs to be financed by the state are all essential parts of this agenda. The pandemic has demonstrated the crucial role the state needs to play in shaping and implementing policies that move us toward a healthier, more stable, more equitable, and more sustainable outcome for all. It has also demonstrated the need for compassion as a core value and a core practice that must guide our actions and our policies.

I am reminded of my mother, a retired math and science high school teacher, who has impacted the lives of countless children during the more than 30 years that she taught at our local school in Mumbai. As a teacher she earned a very modest sum of money with no retirement or health benefits, demonstrating how little we value her contributions in the care economy. Recently several students my mother taught came together and decided to reach out to their teachers, without whom they would not be who and where they are now. They started by asking the teachers what they needed in terms of financial assistance, medical support, emotional support, or other things to feel acknowledged and cherished for their invaluable contributions. It is time that we followed the same practice by asking those who contribute to the flourishing and sustaining of life what they need and how they would like to be compensated and valued.

Invitation to reflect: Take a moment to reflect on someone in your life who cared for you and helped you become who you are today. If you could, how might you express gratitude to this person?

Key Takeaways

Below are the key ideas to take away from this chapter:

- Starting with the Truman doctrine, the concept of development was socially constructed by using the economic model of rapid economic growth and industrialization that developed in the United States and in Western Europe as the golden standard to which all countries must aspire regardless of specific historical, social, cultural, and economic conditions existing in these countries.
- There has been mounting empirical evidence that demonstrates that economic growth does not always lead to greater well-being, challenging one of the most basic assumptions of economics as a discipline.
- Seligman defines well-being as multifaceted human flourishing. These facets include positive affect, engagement, relationships and social support, meaning and purpose, and accomplishment and autonomy.
- Sen defines development as an expansion of entitlements and the capabilities that these entitlements generate to live in ways that we value.
- Feminist economists see development as a process that provides for the survival, sustenance, and flourishing of life.

Comprehension Questions

Directions: Use what you have learned in this chapter to help you respond to the questions below:

- What is the concept of development constructed by the Truman doctrine? Why and under what conditions did this particular conceptualization of development occur?
- What is the Easterlin paradox, and why is it important to the study of the economics of development?
- What is the conceptualization of development constructed by Sen? How is it different from the one constructed by the Truman doctrine?
- What is the conceptualization of development constructed by feminist economists? How is it different from the one constructed by the Truman doctrine?

References

Beneria, L. (2003). *Gender, development, and globalization: Economics as if people mattered*. Routledge.
Brickman, P., & Campbell, D. (1971). Hedonic relativism and planning the good society. In M. H. Appley (Ed.), *Adaptation level theory*. Academic Press.
Deci, E. L., & Ryan, R. M. (2000). The "what" and "why" of goal pursuits: Human needs and the self-determination of behavior. *Psychological Inquiry*, 11(4), 227– 268. http://dx.doi.org/10.1207/S15327965PLI1104_01
Diener, E. & Seligman, M.E. (2004.) Beyond Money: Toward an Economy of Well-Being. Psychological Science in the Public Interest, 5, 1-31. http://dx.doi.org/10.1111/j.0963-7214.2004.00501001.x
Diener, E., Wirtz, D., Tov, W., Kim-Prieto, C., Choi, D.-W., Oishi, S., & Biswas-Diener, R. (2010). New well-being measures: Short scales to assess flourishing and positive and negative feelings. *Social Indicators Research*, 97, 143–156. http://dx.doi.org/10.1007/s11205-009-9493-y
Easterlin, R. (1974). Does economic growth improve the human lot? Some empirical evidence. In P. David & W. Melvin (Eds.), *Nations and households in economic growth* (pp. 89–125). Stanford University Press.
Easterlin, R. (2005). Building a better theory of well-being. In L. Bruni & P. Porta (Eds.), *Economics and happiness: Framing the analysis* (pp. 29–64). Oxford University Press.
Escobar, A. (1995). *Encountering development*. Princeton University Press.
Ferber, M. & Nelson, J. (Eds.). (1993). *Beyond economic man: Feminist theory and economics*. Chicago University Press.
Floro, M. (1995). Women's well-being, poverty, and work intensity. *Feminist Economics*, 1(3), 1–25.
Folbre, N. (1994). *Who pays for the kids? Gender and the structures of constraint*. Routledge.
Lucas, R., Clark, A., Georgellis, Y., & Diener, E. (2003). Reexamining adaptation and the set point model of happiness: Reactions to change in marital status. *Journal of Personality and Social Psychology*, 84, 527–539.
Lyubomirsky, S., King, L., & Diener, E. (2005). The benefits of frequent positive affect: Does happiness lead to success? *Psychological Bulletin*, 131, 803–855.
Mohanty, C. (1991). Under Western eyes: Feminist scholarship and colonial discourses. In C. Mohanty, A. Russo & L. Torres (Eds.), *Third World women and the politics of feminism* (pp. 51–80). Indiana University Press.
Mudimbe, V. (1988). *The Invention of Africa*. Indiana University Press.
Nelson, J., & Power, M. (2018). Ecology, Sustainability, and Care: Developments in the Field. *Feminist Economics* 24(3), 80-88.
Nussbaum, M. (2003). Capabilities as fundamental entitlements: Sen and social justice. *Feminist Economics*, 9(2/3), 33–60.
Power, M. (2004). Social provisioning as a starting point for feminist economics. *Feminist Economics*, 10(3), 3–19.
Rai, S. (2011). The history of international development: Concepts and contexts. In N. Visvanathan, L. Duggan, N. Wiegersma & L. Nisonoff (Eds.), *The women, gender and development reader* (2nd ed., pp. 14–21). Zed Books.
Rawls, J. (1971). *A theory of justice*. Belknap Press.
Reis, H., & Gable, S. (2003). Toward a positive psychology of relationships. In C. L. M. Keyes & J. Haidt (Eds.), Flourishing: *Positive psychology and the life well-lived* (pp. 129–159). American Psychological Association. http://dx.doi.org/10.1037/10594-006
Said, E. (1979) *Orientalism*. Vintage Books.
Seligman, M. (2011). *Flourish*. Simon & Schuster.
Sen, A. (1999). *Development as freedom*. Alfred A Knopf.
Sheldon, K., & Lyubomirsky, S. (2006). Achieving sustainable gains in happiness: Change your actions, not your circumstances. *Journal of Happiness Studies*, 7 (1), 55–86.
Sugden, R. (2006). Correspondence of sentiments. In L. Bruni & P. Porta (Eds.), *Economics and happiness: Framing the analysis* (pp. 91–115). Oxford University Press.
UN Women. (2021). Beyond Covid-19: *A feminist plan for sustainability and social justice*. Research and Data Section, UN Women.
Zamagni, S. (2006). Happiness and individualism. In L. Bruni & P. Porta (Eds.), *Economics and happiness: Framing the analysis* (pp. 303–335). Oxford University Press.

Chapter 3

Measures of Economic Development

> What you measure affects what you do. If you don't measure the right thing, you don't do the right thing.
>
> —Nobel laureate Joseph Stiglitz, American economist
> (as cited by Goodman, 2009, para. 3)

From Local Stories to Global Visions

The country of Bhutan has developed its own measure of development called Gross National Happiness (GNH) based on the four pillars of good governance, sustainable socioeconomic development, cultural preservation, and environmental conservation. The four pillars have been further divided into nine domains: psychological well-being, health, education, time use, cultural diversity and resilience, good governance, community vitality, ecological diversity and resilience, and living standards. By not using GDP per capita as their sole measure of development, the policies they have implemented to maximize GNH instead are very different from those of other countries. For example, they use economic principles to internalize the externalities imposed by tourism by collecting a hefty fee from all tourists. While this fee deters many tourists from going to Bhutan, it has also led to Bhutan being the only country in the world that has actually increased its forest cover during the last 50 years.

Invitation to reflect: Take a moment to reflect on factors that you would include if you could design your own measure of development.

Introduction

Chapter 2 provided a broadly accepted and shared understanding of different concepts of development from a social justice perspective. We focused on the economic growth approach, the well-being approach, the capabilities approach, and the feminist approach. In this chapter, we focus on measures of development that spring from each of these conceptualizations of development. The measures arising out of each of the four approaches we discussed in chapter 2 are listed below in table 1.

Table 3.1 Measures Associated with Each Development Approach

Approach to development	Measures
Economic Growth approach	GDP per capita
Well-being approach	Subjective measures such as life ladder, life satisfaction, U-index. Objective measures such as quality of life indicators, basic needs, social progress indicators.
Capabilities approach	Human Development Index (HDI), Gender Development Index (GDI), Planetary pressure adjusted HDI (PHDI)
Feminist approach	Genuine Progress Indicator (GPI)

In the words of American politician, Robert Kennedy (1968):

> The GNP does not allow for the health of our children, the quality of their education, or the joy of their play. It does not include the beauty of our poetry or the strength of our marriages, the intelligence of our public debate or the integrity of our public officials. It measures everything, in short, except that which makes life worthwhile.

The discussion about development has often focused on problems of measurement. Over time we chose to focus only on that which we can easily measure, which then became what we funded and prioritized, not because they were the most important but because we could measure them. Recent challenges to this approach have led to the creation of more measures and to the discussion of alternative ways of prioritizing and funding that are not based on "easy" or staid measurement alone. In this chapter we will define and discuss different ways of measuring development and the implications of using each of these measures.

Measuring Economic Growth

Economic growth is measured as the percent of change in real gross domestic product (GDP) per capita. Real GDP is the inflation-adjusted value of all final goods and services produced in a country in a given period, usually a year. It is important to remember that a country's GDP does not provide a measure of all productive activities in a country, nor does it tell us how the output is distributed across the population. Rising inequality highlights the need for a measure that captures the way resources are distributed. GDP excludes unpaid work, such as volunteer work or most of the work done in the home. It also excludes much of the harmful environmental impact of our actions. Having said that economic growth does give us a broad understanding of changes in particular aspects of the economy over time. For example, the data in table 2 reveals the pre-pandemic growth rate in selected countries around the world, followed by the dramatic reduction in economic output during 2020 and then the recovery in 2021.

Table 3.2 Annual Percentage Growth Rate of GDP per Capita

Region/Country	2019	2020	2021
World	1.26%	-4.58%	5.9%
Australia	0.62%	-1.53%	2.2%
Brazil	0.65%	-4.74%	4.6%
China	5.57%	1.98%	8.1%
Costa Rica	1.19%	-5.41%	7.6%
European Union	1.49%	-6.32%	5.4%
India	2.99%	-8.87%	8.7%
Mexico	-1.14%	-9.20%	4.7%
Sri Lanka	1.63%	-4.08%	3.3%
South Africa	-1.16%	-8.14%	4.9%
United States	1.69%	-3.82%	5.9%

Source: World Bank national accounts data, and OECD National Accounts data files.

The data reveals that not all countries experienced the pandemic contraction in output in the same way. Countries such as Mexico, India, and South Africa suffered a major decline in output, followed closely by the European Union. Countries such as the United States, Brazil, and Costa Rica were in the midrange, and China did not experience a decline at all. However, these numbers hide the differential impact on output within a country. We estimate that inequality within countries has increased during this time in most countries around the world. Those industries that were able to pivot to virtual operations more easily were able to minimize the impact of the pandemic. In addition, the significant pressures on the care economy (and subsequently on women) brought on by the pandemic is largely un(der)counted in GDP calculations, which further highlights the shortcomings of using GDP as the sole measure of development.

Invitation to reflect: Take a moment to reflect on different activities that you have engaged in today and consider which of those activities are included in the GDP and which ones are excluded.

Measuring Well-Being

As mentioned earlier, there has been growing discontent with economic growth as the sole measure of human well-being, but we did not have consistent measures of well-being until a couple of decades ago. Several measures of well-being have been developed over the last two decades, and these have been tested by psychologists and found to be reasonably reliable and consistent. Researchers have found that physiological indicators are fairly consistent with self-reported measures of well-being. These measures allow for interpersonal comparison because most people care about the same three things: economic situation, family and social connections, and health. In specific terms, these factors might mean different things to different people across different cultures and life circumstances, but the groupings are the same.

Invitation to reflect: Take a moment to reflect on your own life and consider what your life would have to be like for you to be completely happy.

Subjective Measures of Well-Being

Measures can be broadly classified into subjective and objective measures of well-being. Subjective measures of well-being ask people about their direct experience of happiness or positive affect (Diener et al., 2010). Subjective measures of well-being can be further classified into evaluative measures and experiential measures. A widely used evaluative measure of subjective well-being used in the World Happiness Report, published annually since 2012, is the ladder of life question. People are asked to evaluate and rate their lives on a ladder of life scale from 0 to 10 where 0 is the worst possible life and 10 is the best possible life.

Invitation to reflect: Take a moment to reflect on your own life and consider which step of the ladder you feel you stand on at this time.

The data in table 3 reveal the rankings and three-year average Cantril ladder scores from 2019–2021. According to the World Happiness Report (Helliwell et al., 2022), Finland, Denmark, and Iceland continue to be the three happiest countries in the world, whereas Afghanistan is the least happy country. Not surprisingly, these rankings mirror the global gender gap index rankings discussed in chapter 1.

Table 3.3 Ranking of Happiness Averaged over 2019–2021

Region/Country	**Ranking**	**Average ladder score**
Finland	1	7.82
Denmark	2	7.64
Iceland	3	7.56
Australia	12	7.16
United States	16	6.98
Brazil	38	6.29

Table 3.3 Ranking of Happiness Averaged over 2019–2021

Mexico	46	6.13
China	72	5.58
South Africa	91	5.19
India	136	3.78
Afghanistan	146	2.40

World Happiness Report 2022 based on Gallup World Poll data.

The Day Reconstruction Method (DRM), developed by Israeli-born American psychologist and Nobel Prize winner Daniel Kahneman and others, is an example of an experiential measure of subjective well-being (Kahneman et al., 2004). I have used the DRM in my own research with my colleague American psychologist Marie Thomas on the well-being of women working in the informal labor market in Mumbai, India (Basu & Thomas, 2009). In 2008 we interviewed more than 200 women working in four different occupations: street vendors, homebased workers, domestic workers, and construction workers. We asked them to break down the previous day of their lives into 20 to 30-minute episodes. We then asked them to identify the frequency and intensity of positive and negative emotions they experienced during the episodes. We used the DRM to calculate the U-index, which is the proportion of time spent in an unhappy state, during which the highest rated emotion was a negative one. Some of our findings are summarized in table 4.

Table 3.4 U-Index and Average Monthly Income of Women Working in Informal Labor Market in Mumbai

	U-Index	**Average monthly income**
Domestic workers	24%	Rs. 1,811
Construction workers	28%	Rs. 1,423
Street vendors	25%	Rs. 1,551
Homebased workers	16%	Rs. 840

We found that even though the homebased workers had the lowest income, they also had the lowest U-index because they had more flexibility, more autonomy, and less direct supervision. A majority of the wage workers (domestic workers and construction workers) wanted better jobs in the formal sector. Major barriers for them were lack of education, lack of social capital, household/childcare responsibilities, and lack of jobs. Construction workers and domestic workers in particular, reported that sexual harassment and assault in the worksite was rampant and needed urgent attention. Self-employed workers (street vendors and homebased workers) did not want jobs in the formal sector. They wanted better access to credit, access to safer workspaces and better infrastructure. All of them wanted access to potable water. Our research revealed the importance of considering other measures of well-being beyond income to get a better understanding of what people need to improve their lives.

Many studies combine evaluative and experiential measures of well-being to understand different aspects of well-being. I have used this approach in my collaborative research on the well-being of college students (Basu & Thomas, 2019). We surveyed more than 500 students and used their responses to calculate the U-index (experiential measure) and the overall life satisfaction (evaluative measure). The overall life satisfaction measure continues to be another widely used evaluative measure of subjective well-being. The simplicity and ease of this measure is one of its primary attractions. This measure involves asking a single question: Taking all things together, how satisfied are you with your life as a whole these days? Your answer can range from very satisfied to not at all satisfied. These two measures capture different aspects of well-being. Students have to work hard and stay up nights studying, which might not be pleasurable in the Benthamite sense (U-index) but when done well brings a sense of satisfaction akin to Aristotle's eudaimonia (life satisfaction) conceptualization of happiness. Our findings are summarized in table 5.

Table 3.5 Correlations Between U-index, Life Satisfaction, and Demographic/Academic Variables

Variable	**Correlation with U-index**	**Correlation with life satisfaction**
Grade point average	0.017	0.121*
Hours worked per week	-0.076	-0.002
Number of units enrolled	0.029	-0.006
Hours slept night before	-0.286*	0.109*
Percentage of college costs paid by family	0.029	0.126*

**Statistically significant*

We found that the correlation between life satisfaction and GPA is statistically significant, but the correlation with the U-index is not. Hours worked per week and number of college units was not significant for either measure, while the correlation with hours slept the night before taking the survey was statistically significant with both measures.

Objective Measures of Well-Being

Efforts have also been made to develop national indicators of well-being that can inform policy decisions. Most of these indicators have been objective measures of well-being. Rawls (1971) was one of the first to identify a set of primary goods that he determined to be necessary for a good life. The basic needs theory (Doyal & Gough, 1991) was a similar approach that identified health and autonomy as the most important basic needs for human beings and included a list of conditions necessary to achieving these two needs. A more recent approach (Narayan-Parker, 2000) is based on compiling a list of needs identified by focus groups from low-income countries. This approach called the *Voices of the Poor* analysis addresses some of the concerns about so-called objective measures by directly asking those whose needs we are trying to ascertain to voice their needs. Several countries have also come up with their own social indicators or quality of life indicators. For example, the report by the Commission on the Measurement of Economic Performance and Social Progress" (CMEPSP), created by French President Nicholas Sarkozy in 2008, made several recommendations for a better measure of social and economic progress (Stiglitz et al., 2009). These recommendations include broadening the scope of GDP to include nonmarket activities and focusing on the distribution of income and consumption at the household level. They also recommended a multifaceted approach to measuring well-being, which included the following: (a) material living conditions (income, consumption, and wealth); (b) health; (c) education; (d) personal activities (including work); (e) political participation; (f) social connections and relationships; (g) environmental conditions; (h) insecurity.

Measuring Capabilities

It is hard to measure human development according to the capability approach and even harder to make comparisons across countries because it involves value judgments regarding which capabilities are valuable. But certain capabilities could be judged as universal, such as the ability to live a healthy life, the ability to be well-nourished, and the ability to control our lives and work conditions. Lack of development can then be defined as the failure to have certain minimum capabilities that can be defined as absolute.

An attempt has been made by the United Nations Development Program (UNDP) to measure development as an expansion of capabilities. Since there is considerable disagreement about whether we can identify a universal set of freedoms or capabilities, this index only relies on three measures, namely real gross national income (GNI) per capita, life expectancy, and adult literacy. For each of these, a relative deprivation measure is calculated in terms of how far the country is from the highest amount possible. The same procedure is followed for all three indicators, and then the three are averaged to calculate the average amount of deprivation. Then it is subtracted from one to give a measure of human development, which can take a maximum value of one and a minimum value of zero. This measure is a relative measure and only Indicates a ranking of countries in relation to another. The human development index (HDI) for selected countries for 2021–2022 are listed in table 6.

Table 3.6 HDI and Its Components for 2021–2022

Country	Life expectancy at birth	Expected years of schooling	Gross national income per capita (PPP)	Human development index	HDI Rank
Switzerland	84	16.5	$66,933	0.962	1
Norway	83.2	18.2	$64,660	0.961	2
Iceland	82.7	19.2	$55,782	0.959	3
Australia	84.5	21.1	$49,238	0.951	5
United States	77.2	16.3	$64,765	0.921	21
Costa Rica	77	16.5	$19,974	0.809	57
Sri Lanka	76.4	14.1	$12,578	0.782	73
China	78.2	14.2	$17,504	0.768	79
Mexico	70.2	14.9	$17,896	0.758	86

Table 3.6 HDI and Its Components for 2021–2022

Brazil	72.8	15.6	$14,370	0.754	87
South Africa	62.3	13.6	$12,948	0.713	109
India	67.2	11.9	$6,590	0.633	132
Afghanistan	62	10.3	$1,824	0.478	180

Source: Human Development Report 2021–22, UNDP

The numbers reveal that the HDI ranking and the GNI per capita ranking are not the same. United States has a higher GNI per capita ranking than Australia but has a lower HDI ranking. Sri Lanka has a lower GNI per capita ranking than China but a higher HDI ranking. According to the Human Development Report (2021–22), rising uncertainties brought about by the pandemic, climate change, rising inequality, war and economic crises has led to a second consecutive year of decline in the global human development index. The global HDI has dropped from 0.739 in 2019 to 0.735 in 2020 to 0.732 in 2021. This unprecedented decline in the human development index for almost every country in the world has never occurred in the 32 years that the HDI has been measured.

The HDI has been adjusted for inequality and calculated separately for men and women. The gender development index is the ratio of female to male HDI values. The world GDI is 0.958 with the world HDI for women at 0.715 and the world HDI for men at 0.747. The GDI for selected countries for 2021–2022 is listed in table 7. For most countries, this ratio is less than one, but a few countries have achieved gender parity, such as Ukraine, Thailand, United States, Vietnam, Uruguay, Namibia, and Qatar. Much of the gains in gender parity have been achieved in life expectancy and years of schooling. The gender gap in GNI per capita continues to persist such that there is no country that has achieved parity in average GNI per capita.

Table 3.7 Gender Development Index for 2021–2022

Country	**Gender development index**	**Expected GNI per capita for women**	**Expected GNI per capita for men**
Norway	0.983	$54,699	$74,445
Australia	0.968	$37,486	$61,161
United States	1.001	$51,539	$78,238
Costa Rica	0.996	$16,568	$23,376
Sri Lanka	0.949	$7,005	$18,573
Mexico	0.989	$12,456	$23,600
Brazil	0.994	$10,903	$17,960
China	0.984	$13,980	$20,883

Table 3.7 Gender Development Index for 2021–2022

South Africa	0.944	$9,935	$16,129
India	0.849	$2,277	$10,633
Afghanistan	0.681	$533	$3,089

Source: Human Development Report 2021–22, UNDP

In 2021, UNDP adjusted the original HDI to include the impact of planetary pressures to create the PHDI. The adjustment factor is calculated as the arithmetic mean of indices measuring carbon dioxide emissions per capita and material footprint per capita. When the world HDI of 0.732 is adjusted for planetary pressures, it gives us a world PHDI of 0.667. If a country puts no pressure on the planet, then its PHDI and its HDI are the same. As the planetary pressure increases, the PHDI drops below the HDI, which changes the rankings of the countries. The PHDI for selected countries for 2021–2022 is presented in table 8. If the change in ranking is negative, then it indicates that the planetary pressure is high enough that its PHDI dropped relative to other countries.

Table 3.8 Planetary Pressure Adjusted HDI (PHDI) for 2021–2022

Country	PHDI	Change in Ranking
Norway	0.734	-34
Australia	0.637	-87
United States	0.698	-36
Costa Rica	0.746	+26
Sri Lanka	0.761	+46
Mexico	0.704	+21
Brazil	0.676	+5
China	0.648	-14
South Africa	0.648	+6
India	0.609	+6

Source: Human Development Report 2021–22, UNDP

The numbers reveal that most high-income countries have a larger planetary impact and therefore their PHDI results in a loss in HDI ranking. For example, countries such as Costa Rica, Sri Lanka, and Mexico have a higher PHDI than the United States. These numbers suggest that overconsumption is a bigger problem for sustainable development than underconsumption.

Measures of Sustainable Development

In September 2015, the General Assembly of the United Nations adopted the 2030 Agenda for Sustainable Development with its 17 sustainable development goals (SDGs) and 169 targets and measures at the UN Sustainable Development Summit in New York. Sustainable development has three dimensions: social, economic, and environmental.

The SDGs are listed as follows:

- Goal 1: End extreme poverty measured in part by those who are living on less than $1.25 per day. The pandemic has resulted in the first rise in extreme poverty in 20 years with an additional 119 to 124 million people pushed into poverty. A number of countries have instituted social protection measures, but 4 billion people are still not covered by any social protection measures.
- Goal 2: End world hunger measured in part as those who are without food or are unable to eat a healthy balanced diet on a regular basis (2.37 billion people in 2020). The pandemic has exacerbated world hunger, and it is estimated that an additional 82 to 132 million people experienced chronic hunger in 2020.
- Goal 3: Ensure healthy lives for all measured in a variety of ways from child mortality rates to reproductive health. Before the pandemic we were making significant progress toward this goal, but it is estimated that the pandemic has reversed many of these gains.
- Goal 4: Ensure inclusive and equitable quality education for all, measured in part as the number of children who have access to free, quality, and equitable primary and secondary education, resulting in effective learning outcomes. The pandemic has wiped out 20 years of progress with an additional 101 million children falling below minimum reading proficiency levels in 2020. Roughly two-thirds of children continue to be affected by school closures with the most vulnerable never returning to school and being forced into child labor or child marriages. The impact on education has been one of the most catastrophic outcomes of COVID-19 that will continue to play out for generations to come.
- Goal 5: Achieve gender equality and empower all women and girls measured in a variety of ways from gender gaps in wages, mortality rates, education, health, nutrition, political participation to violence against women. The pandemic has wiped out decades of progress towards gender equality with women bearing the brunt of additional care work, increased exposure to the virus due to their disproportionate numbers among essential workers, greater job loss and increase in domestic violence and child marriages. It is estimated that an additional 10 million girls will be at risk of child marriage over the next decade. One in three women have experienced sexual or physical violence at least once since the age of 15 and this number is estimated to have increased during the pandemic.
- Goal 6: Ensure availability and sustainable management of water and sanitation for all measured in a variety of ways. For example, one in three people worldwide still lack basic handwashing facilities at home, leaving them especially vulnerable to the COVID-19 virus. Between 1970 and 2015, wetlands decreased by 35%, and they continue to decrease at an alarming rate.
- Goal 7: Ensure access to affordable, reliable, sustainable, and modern energy for all measured in a variety of ways. For example, while global access to electricity has increased, 759 million people still do not have access to electricity. One third of the world's population still uses unhealthy and

dangerous cooking systems. Only 9.2% of the heat sector and 3.4% of the transport sector uses modern renewable energy.

- Goal 8: Promote inclusive and sustainable economic growth, full and productive employment, and decent work for all measured in a variety of ways. For example, the pandemic resulted in the equivalent of 255 million full-time jobs lost in 2020. The pandemic has led to an increase in the number of young people who are unemployed or not in school or training. Tourism was one of the hardest hit sectors with international arrivals down 74% in 2020, resulting in over a 100 million jobs lost in the tourism sector alone.
- Goal 9: Build resilient infrastructure, promote inclusive and sustainable industrialization measured in a variety of ways. For example, the pandemic resulted in an 8.4% drop in manufacturing output globally, causing supply-chain disruptions across the world. Small-scale businesses were hard hit, and many of them were unable to survive the pandemic.
- Goal 10: Reduce inequality within and among countries measured in a variety of ways, including the GINI index. The GINI index ranges from 0 to 100 where 0 means that income is equally shared and 100 means that 1 person accounts for all the income. It is estimated that the pandemic has increased the GINI index by 6% for emerging and developing countries. Rising inequality continues to be one of the major challenges we face over the next few decades.
- Goal 11: Make cities and human settlements inclusive, safe, resilient, and sustainable, measured by equitable access to housing, basic services, air quality, public transport, and open spaces. More than 1 billion people continue to live in slum dwellings with limited access to basic services, and only half of the world's urban population had access to public transport, which was exacerbated by the pandemic and closure of public transport systems.
- Goal 12: Ensure sustainable consumption and production patterns measured in a variety of ways. For example, the global material footprint increased by 70% between 2000 and 2017. While the pandemic led to a decrease in world consumption and production, it is estimated that we will return to pre-pandemic levels very quickly unless we choose to do things differently.
- Goal 13: Take urgent action to combat climate change and its impacts measured by the number of actions taken by member countries and the resulting outcomes. Climate change continues virtually unabated, but 125 low and medium-income countries are in the process of formulating and implementing climate adaptation policies.
- Goal 14: Conserve and sustainably use the oceans, seas, and marine resources measured in a variety of ways. Our oceans continue to be under severe threat from global warming, fishery collapses, pollution, and acidification. Dead zones, defined as areas of water with insufficient oxygen to support marine life, have been increasing dramatically from 400 in 2008 to 700 in 2019. Over 3 billion people rely on the oceans for their livelihoods, and it is critical that we conserve and protect our marine resources.
- Goal 15: Protect, restore, and promote sustainable use of natural resources measured in a variety of ways. For example, we have lost over 100 million hectares of forestland over the last two decades. More than 37,400 species are threatened by extinction, which represents a 10% increase over the last three decades. We have made some efforts in this area, but we have to do much more to prevent continued deforestation and loss of biodiversity.
- Goal 16: Provide access to justice for all and build effective, accountable, and inclusive institutions

measured in a variety of ways. We are far from achieving this goal, and millions of people, especially children, continue to live in conflict zones and areas around the world with high threat of violence. The pandemic has resulted in higher rates of child trafficking and child labor. Child labor rose, for the first time in two decades, to 160 million.

- Goal 17: Strengthen the means of implementation and revitalize global partnerships measured in a variety of ways. For example, Overseas Development Assistance (ODA) reached a record high of $161 billion in 2020. Remittance flows to medium and low-income countries fell slightly but still remained at $540 billion as compared to $548 billion in 2019. Foreign direct investment fell by 40% due to slow and often negative economic growth in most parts of the world. In terms of connectivity, 3.7 billion people, representing over half of the world's population, do not have access to the internet, highlighting the need for investment in communication infrastructure.

Invitation to reflect: Take a moment to reflect on which of these goals resonated with you the most and what you, in a small way, might do to help us reach that goal.

Measures of Feminist Development

The task of accounting for and making visible women's unpaid work has been underway since the 1970s. Feminist economists have discussed the methodological and measurement issues inherent in valuating unpaid work and have called for systematic time use surveys and satellite accounts of household labor (Waring, 2003; Benería et al., 2015). American economist Gunseli Berik (2018) argues that the Genuine Progress Indicator (GPI) is the best measure available at this time (Cobb et al., 1995, Anielski et al., 1999), even though it has limitations because it addresses the concerns of feminist economists with regard to the invisibility of unpaid work and it addresses the concerns of ecological economists with regard to the invisibility of ecosystems. As described by Berik (2018, pg. 3),

> GPI is a composite indicator that incorporates roughly 25 adjustments to personal consumption expenditures, the largest component of GDP. It weights personal consumption by income inequality, incorporates both the value of non-market activities and the social and environmental costs associated with market activity. All components of GPI are expressed in monetary units and aggregated into a single GPI value, akin to the GDP.

The GPI addresses concerns about income inequality, climate change, and the invisibility of unpaid work and the care economy. It has been calculated for more than 28 countries at the national level and several other cities and states at a subnational level. A study of 17 countries found that real GDP per capita and real GPI per capita are highly correlated till about $7,000 real GDP per capita (Kubiszewski et al., 2013). After that, real GDP per capita keeps increasing but real GPI per capita remains flat or falls as the real environmental costs of growth offset the benefits of growth. When states or cities adopt renewable energy policies that reduce the environmental costs of growth, they can again achieve rising real GPI per capita.

Some feminist economists resist the idea of any one measure capturing the social provisioning and conditions necessary for the sustenance and flourishing of life (Dobell & Walsh, 2013). They prefer narratives and building of social consensus as a means to move the agenda of feminist development forward.

Key Takeaways

Below are the key ideas to take away from this chapter:

- Measurement issues have led us to focus on that which we can easily measure, which then became what we funded and prioritized. Recent challenges to this approach have led to the creation of more measures and to the discussion of alternative ways of prioritizing and funding that are not based on measurement alone.
- Economic growth is measured as the percentage change in real gross domestic product (GDP) per capita. It is important to remember that a country's GDP does not provide a measure of all productive activities in a country, nor does it tell us how the output is distributed across the population.
- Several measures of well-being have been developed over the last two decades and these have been tested by psychologists and found to be reasonably reliable and consistent.
- It is hard to measure human development according to the capability approach because it must involve value judgments regarding which capabilities are valuable. But there are certain capabilities that could be judged as universal, such as the ability to live a healthy life, the ability to be well-nourished, and the ability to control our lives and work conditions.
- Some feminist economists resist the idea of any one measure capturing the social provisioning and conditions necessary for the sustenance and flourishing of life. They prefer narratives and building of social consensus as a means to move the agenda of feminist development forward.

Comprehension Questions

Directions: Use what you have learned in this chapter to help you respond to the questions below:

- What can you learn from the economic growth measure of development? What are the limitations of this measure?
- In what ways are the measures of well-being different from the economic growth measure of development?
- In what ways are the indices that measure capabilities different from the economic growth measure of development?
- In what ways are the measures of feminist development different from the economic growth measure of development?
- How does each measure of development help you understand your own well-being and that of the community to which you belong? How do they influence the kind of policies you might implement to improve the well-being of your community?

References

Anielski, M. & Rowe, J. (1999). The Genuine Progress Indicator—1998 Update (San Francisco, Redefining Progress).
Basu, R., & Thomas, M. (2009). Exploring women's daily lives and participation in the informal labour market in Mumbai, India. *Gender & Development,* 17(2), 231–242, DOI: 10.1080/13552070903009791
Basu, R. & Thomas, M. (2019). What makes college students happy? A day reconstruction study. In S. Bushey, B. Martin, M. Cihan Camci, & S. Klausen (Eds.), *Perspectives on happiness* (pp. 29-40). Brill Publishers.
Benería, L., Berik, G., & Floro, M. (2015). Gender, development, and globalization: Economics as if all people mattered (2nd ed.). Routledge.
Berik, G. (2018). *Towards more inclusive measures of economic well-being: Debates and practices* (ILO Future of Work Research Paper Series 2). International Labour Organization.
Cobb, C., Halstead, T., & Rowe, J. (1995). If the GDP is up, why is America down? *The Atlantic Monthly,* 276, 59–78.
Deci, E. L., & Ryan, R. M. (2000). The "what" and "why" of goal pursuits: Human needs and the self-determination of behavior. *Psychological Inquiry, 11,* 227–268. http://dx.doi.org/10.1207/S15327965PLI1104_01
Diener, E., Wirtz, D., Tov, W., Kim-Prieto, C., Choi, D.-W., Oishi, S., & Biswas-Diener, R. (2010). New well-being measures: Short scales to assess flourishing and positive and negative feelings. *Social Indicators Research, 97,* 143–156. http://dx.doi.org/10.1007/s11205-009-9493-y
Dobell, R., & Walsh, J. (2013). Narrative trumps numbers: Marilyn Waring in the world. In M. Bjornholt & A. McKay (Eds.), *Counting on Marilyn Waring: New advances in feminist economics* (pp. 139–155). Demeter Press.
Doyal, L., & Gough, I. (1991). *A theory of human need.* MacMillan.
Goodman, P. (2009, September 23). Emphasis on growth is called misguided. *The New York Times.*
Helliwell, J. F., Layard, R., Sachs, J. D., De Neve, J.-E., Aknin, L. B., & Wang, S. (Eds.). (2022). *World Happiness Report 2022.* New York: Sustainable Development Solutions Network.
Kahneman, D., Krueger, A., Schkade, D., Schwarz, N., & Stone, A. (2004). A survey method for characterizing daily life experiences: The day reconstruction method. *Science, 306,* 1776–1780. http://dx.doi.org/10.1126/science.1103572
Kubiszewski, I., Costanza, R., Carol, F., Lawn, P., Talberth, J., Jackson, T., & Aylmer, C. (2013). Beyond GDP: Measuring and achieving global genuine progress. *Ecological Economics,* 93, 57–68.
Lucas, R., Clark, A., Georgellis, Y., & Diener, E. (2003). Reexamining adaptation and the set point model of happiness: Reactions to change in marital status. *Journal of Personality and Social Psychology, 84,* 527–539.
Narayan-Parker, D. (2000). *Crying out for change: Voices of the poor.* Oxford University Press for the World Bank. http://dx.doi.org/10.1596/0-1952-1602-4
Rawls, J. (1971). A theory of justice. Belknap Press.
Stiglitz J., Sen, A., & Fitoussi, J. (2009). *Report of the commission on the measurement of economic performance and social progress.*
UNDP (United Nations Development Programme). (2022). *Human development report 2021–22: Uncertain times, unsettled lives: Shaping our future in a transforming world.* New York.
Waring, M. (2003). Counting for something! Recognizing women's contribution to the global economy through alternative accounting systems. *Gender and Development,* 11(1), 35–43.

Chapter 4

Gender and Theories of Development

> Today we no longer say: "give us more jobs, more rights, consider us your equals or even allow us to compete with you better." But rather: let us reexamine the whole question, all the questions. Let us take nothing for granted. Let us not only redefine ourselves, our role, our image—but also the kind of society we want to live in.
>
> —*In Search of Answers: Indian Women's Voices* (Kishwar & Vanita, Eds., 1984)

From Local Stories to Global Visions

In 2021, the Supreme Court of India set precedent when it awarded compensation to the family of a deceased couple who had been hit by a car in 2014, based not only on the income of the man who worked for pay but also the unpaid housework activities of the woman. Justice Ramana referred to recent data that revealed that women in India spend on average 299 minutes a day on unpaid domestic care services, compared to men who spend 97 minutes a day on such activities. "It signals to society at large that the law and courts of the land believe in the value of the labour, services and sacrifices of homemakers. It is an acceptance of the idea that these activities contribute in a very real way to the economic condition of the family and the economy of the nation," the bench said.

Invitation to reflect: Take a moment to reflect on why valuing women's unpaid work is important for gender equality.

Introduction

Chapters 1, 2, and 3 provide a broadly accepted and shared understanding of the concepts of social justice, compassion, and development. In chapter 4 we will focus our attention on the concepts of gender and feminisms. We will discuss the way in which the concepts of gender and the associated concepts of femininity and masculinity have been socially constructed and colonized to justify a global system of oppression. We will focus on how the concept of the "Third World woman" or the "Muslim woman" was constructed by Western feminists based on their own experiences and worldview. We will also analyze how theories and policies of development are gendered and help perpetuate a system of oppression. We will discuss the historical contributions of feminist scholars, activists, and planners to the field of development and the lives of women, men, and children.

Gender as a Historically Produced Discourse

British sociologist and feminist Ann Oakley first introduced the theoretical distinction between the concepts of *sex* and *gender*. According to Oakley (1972), **sex is connected to the biology of our reproductive organs, hormones and other physiological and genetic differences that classify us as being male or female.** On the other hand, **gender is socially, culturally, and historically constructed by a given society.** While this distinction is useful, it can also obfuscate the fact that biological differences themselves are also socially constructed. By placing it within the realm of science, we have intentionally or unintentionally closed the door to further examination of the way in which we have chosen to consider and construct narratives about our bodies and our biology, starting with the assumption of false binaries between men and women. Women's bodies have been and continue to be commodified, sold, violated, and controlled by the courts as recent decisions about abortion rights in the United States have demonstrated.

I recall a story that Jack Kornfield shared during a mindfulness workshop in 2019 that brought home to me the power of social conditioning:

> "Am I gorgeous?" my child asks, drawing the word out like pulled taffy. "Yes," I say, "you are." The pink and teal dress is probably made of some highly flammable material, some chemist's approximation of satin. Pudgy fingers decorated with pink polish trace the sequins on the bodice. "I love this." A giant pair of bubblegum pink wings flap slowly. Little feet dance in sparkly red slippers. "I'm just like a real princess!" "Yes," I say, "you are." Curly hair, joyful smile, flawless skin. This child is the epitome of beauty. This child, my son. He's four years old and prefers to wear dresses. Maybe it's a phase, maybe not. Even as I wonder how I produced such an angelic-looking creature, I wish he would put on some pants and go back to playing with toy tractors. Not because it matters to me—it doesn't, but because I'm already hearing in my head the name-calling he will face in kindergarten. Many adults already seem disturbed by the dresses and utter awkward apologies when they realize he's not female. This culture wants little boys to dream only of baseball, trucks, and trains. This culture has no room for little boys who want to be gorgeous. He picks up a parasol a neighbor gave him and opens it jauntily over his shoulders. "Am I beautiful?" he asks. And I sweep him into my arms and plant a kiss on his cheeks. "Always," I say. "Always."

For me, this story captures the power and all-pervasive nature of social conditioning and the cruelty of social sanctions when people deviate from these gender norms. Most of us conform to these gender norms starting with how we dress to how we act to the kinds of jobs we have. We believe that we are freely choosing these options when in fact they have been chosen for us as we succumb to social norms.

In much academic thinking about the social construction of gender, femininity has been associated with *social reproductive* functions in the private sphere, such as giving birth, but also with caring for the family, managing the household where the requisite skills include nurturing, cooperation, tenderness, and community. On the other hand, social constructions of masculinity have been associated with *productive* functions of being in the public sphere, where the requisite skills include rationality, scientific thinking, and achievement. These gender differences are normatively real and practical, but they are also socially constructed. Men are capable of being nurturing and women are capable of being rational, yet we are socially conditioned and encouraged to develop those traits that match the sex we are assigned at birth.

Invitation to reflect: Take a moment to reflect on the images that come to your mind when you think about the words "femininity" and "masculinity." Reflect on when and how these associations were first formed.

In addition, these skills and/or traits are also valued differently by society. According to German sociologist, Maria Mies (1986), women's labor is seen as being natural, inborn, and unconscious, whereas men's labor is seen as being productive, creative, and rational. We are often told that women are not paid for their domestic caregiving activities because caring for one's family is natural and is part of loving your family. And yet, caregiving work is central to our lives (as has been painfully revealed to us during the pandemic). In a patriarchy/capitalist system, men hold power and control over resources by this sexual division of labor. Men, in general, did the type of work that was considered to create a surplus, whereas women did the type of work that enabled men to go out and create a surplus.

What Is Feminism?

According to Mies, "***Feminists are those who dare to break the conspiracy of silence about the oppressive, unequal man–woman relationship andwho want to change it.***" The women's movement of the 1960s in the United States and Europe gathered momentum as all-women's consciousness raising groups sprang up to openly discuss the oppression that women were experiencing in the home and at the workplace. Women recognized that these experiences were not individual, isolated incidents, but were in fact part of a bigger social and political problem, which created a feeling of sisterhood as the "personal became political." There was often hostile opposition from men in public and private spaces, and "feminism" quickly became a bad word. Both women and men found it difficult to accept that this most intimate of relationships is characterized as oppressive and unequal.

Invitation to reflect: Take a moment to reflect on the images and words that come to mind when you think of the word "feminism." How and when did you make these associations? How do they make you feel?

For very different reasons, women of color in the United States and Europe and from around the world also pushed back against "Western feminism" because these concerns were not universal. They were based on the experiences of white middle-class women. African American scholars such as bell hooks (1981) articulated black feminist thought that questioned the universality of women's experiences and concerns and argued for a more intersectional approach. African American women have faced both racism and sexism and have often had to choose between standing in solidarity with those fighting for the rights of African Americans and those fighting for the rights of women. A classic example is the Black suffrage movement and the Women's suffrage movement in the United States in the 19th century. Black women like Sojourner Truth demanded that voting rights be granted to all people, including both women and people of color. But at that time there was a split between the two movements and ultimately the 15th amendment signed in 1870 focused on race, which gave black men the right to vote but not women. It is true that subsequent measures in the 1890s by different states—such as poll taxes and literacy tests—ended up disenfranchising African American men. But it wasn't until the 19th Amendment was signed in 1920 that most women were granted the same rights. While acknowledging Black patriarchy, Black feminists have wanted to include men in the struggle because the struggle is about race, class, and gender. They also questioned the assumption that women's liberation is based on entering the public sphere of paid employment, especially given the oppressive way that African American women have experienced the workplace. Most African American women were part of the workforce all along, not out of choice, but out of necessity. Consequently, they did not see entering the workforce as a liberating experience.

In a series of international women's conferences convened by the United Nations during the 1970s and 1980s, women came together and started working out their differences to consolidate a feminist agenda. Small groups of women around the world started forming collectives to speak out about the issues they were facing and to look for solutions. Examples include the Sistren Theatre collective, a women's organization established in Jamaica in 1977, committed to using the arts to bring about social change in gender relations. Flora Tristan, established in 1979 in Peru, is another example of a grassroots feminist organization focused on women's rights and gender equality. GELEDÉS Instituto da Mulher Negra, started in Brazil in 1988 is an example of a feminist organization focused on Black women's rights. Saheli was started in 1981 with eight determined women in a garage in Delhi as a crisis intervention center. It is one of the first feminist organizations in India with hundreds of thousands of sahelis (translates to "friend" in English) all over the world. Yewwu-Yewwi, one of the first explicitly feminist organizations in Senegal, was established in 1984 by educated Muslim Senegalese women. It was clear that strengths and weaknesses of the women's movement in the second half of the 20th century were the many divisions between women in terms of ideology from the far left to the far right, in terms of strategy, in terms of geography, in terms of class, sexual orientation, race/ethnicity, religion, caste, and now increasingly gender identity.

Social Construction of the Third World Woman

Indian born, transnational feminist scholar, Chandra Mohanty (1991) discusses the way in which the concept of the *Third World woman* was constructed by Western feminists based on their own experiences and worldview. Third World women were universally considered to be ignorant, backward, and victims of oppression as opposed to First World women who are liberated, forward thinking, and in control over their own lives. According to Mohanty, these labels and characteristics are problematic for several reasons: First, the labels prevent us from understanding the lived reality of women's experiences based on specific social, cultural, and historical conditions. They reduce a multidimensional situation to one dimension. Second, the labels are based on a methodology that sees "Third World women" as objects to be studied and helped versus subjects who have their own agency. Having their own agency implies that they know and can articulate their own needs and wants and are able to resist oppression. Mohanty does not imply that women are not being oppressed or that they don't need help, but rather that to understand somebody else's situation we must respect that they are the best 'knowers' of their own situation. Third, labels constrain and marginalize other ways of thinking about women's concerns in different parts of the world.

More specifically, Palestinian American anthropologist, Lila Abu-Lughod (2011), challenges the social construction of *Muslim women*. She asks why Muslim women need saving. Saving women in Afghanistan was used as one of the justifications for US intervention in Afghanistan. Abu-Lughod questions the feelings of superiority and arrogance that accompany such attempts to save women of color from men of color without any admission or acknowledgement of the oppression that people of color have faced from imperialist powers over the last several centuries. Secondly, saving Muslim women suggests that we see them as being helpless, without agency. Instead, she urges us to accept that while women in different parts of the world want justice, their vision of justice might be very different from what Western feminists might envision for them. Abu-Lughod challenges us, for example, to consider the veil worn by many Muslim women—but not all—from the perspective of the women wearing them. Some Muslim women might consider it a symbol of oppression, but for many it could be an opportunity for mobility in public spaces. Fighting for the removal of the veil might not be their top priority.

The recent protests that started in Iran in 2022 highlight the agency of Iranian women. According to interviews with the protestors, they were protesting the treatment of women by the morality police in Iran. They were protesting the surveilling and controlling of their bodies. They were protesting patriarchy. They weren't protesting the hijab, but rather their right to practice their faith in the way they chose without interference and intimidation from the police.

I remember being at an airport in Paris on my way back to the United States from Mumbai. I was waiting for my connecting flight and felt a chill in the air, which prompted me to cover my head with my scarf. I immediately sensed a change in the way that people perceived me, ranging from fear to pity to suspicion. Abu-Lughod urges us to reflect on our own role in perpetuating stereotypes and contributing to an unjust world order. She challenges us to reflect on how we might give up our own privilege and recognize the rights and agency of women in different part of the world as being the best knowers of their situation.

Invitation to reflect: Take a moment to reflect on what we might do to disrupt stereotypes about Muslim women and give up our own privilege.

Nigerian sociologist and gender scholar Oyeronke Oyewumi (2002) argues that Western feminism is primarily based on the assumption of the nuclear family being the dominant family unit. As a result, Western feminism argues that a woman's identity is based on her role as a wife and all other roles, such as that of being a mother, are secondary to her role as a wife. In many African communities such as the Yoruba community, the nuclear family is not the dominant family unit, and the conjugal relationship is not the primary male–female relationship identifying a woman. In the Yoruba community, kinship ties based on seniority are more important. This does not necessarily mean that women are never oppressed in these communities, but that we would understand female identity and social roles very differently. In other words, it is a mistake to take the assumptions of Western feminism as being universal in all cultures and communities.

Theories of Economic Development

Several theories of development were proffered by mainstream economists seeking to provide a path for low-income countries to follow based on the economic growth approach to economic development discussed in chapter 2. These theories were not simply academic exercises but, in fact, had a profound impact on the lives of millions of people around the world.

Classical Theories

Classical growth theory starts with Adam Smith who argued that the main sources of growth are increases in the labor force and stock of capital, improvements in efficiency with greater division of labor and technological progress and foreign trade. According to Smith, once growth starts it is self-reinforcing, if the growth in wealth favors profits and capital accumulation. With rising capital accumulation, the demand for labor rises and the labor force is absorbed in employment. Division of labor leads to greater efficiency, but division of labor is limited by size of market, making foreign trade important. Rostow's stage theory and Lewis's dual economy theory are two of the most influential theories of development inspired by the classical school of thought.

Rostow's Stage Theory

American economic historian Walt Rostow (1961) argues that it is possible to identify leading sectors in the economy that will propel the economy forward. He believed that development is a linear process that happens in five stages. The first three stages are traditional society, emergence of the preconditions for takeoff, and then the takeoff stage. The takeoff is the central stage and implies a major transition of an economy. The takeoff requires the following preconditions:

- 10% rate of productive investment.
- Development of one or more manufacturing sectors to a high rate of growth.
- Existence of a political, social, and institutional framework that propels and sustains the high rate of growth.

Lewis's Dual Economy Theory

When a dual economy exists, the challenge of development is to expand the modern sector and to contract the traditional sector. Born in the West Indies, Nobel laureate Arthur Lewis (1955) constructed a model of a dual economy with an industrial/capitalist sector and an agricultural/noncapitalist sector. Capitalist sector uses reproducible capital and employs labor for profit-making purposes. It can be public or private. The subsistence sector is a self-employment sector with surplus labor where output per head is low and the marginal productivity of labor may be zero in the *limiting case*. As the capitalist sector expands, it draws labor from the noncapitalist sector at the existing wage. In the subsistence sector, labor is unlimited in some sense and since the marginal productivity is near zero, there is no decline in agricultural output as labor is withdrawn from the subsistence sector.

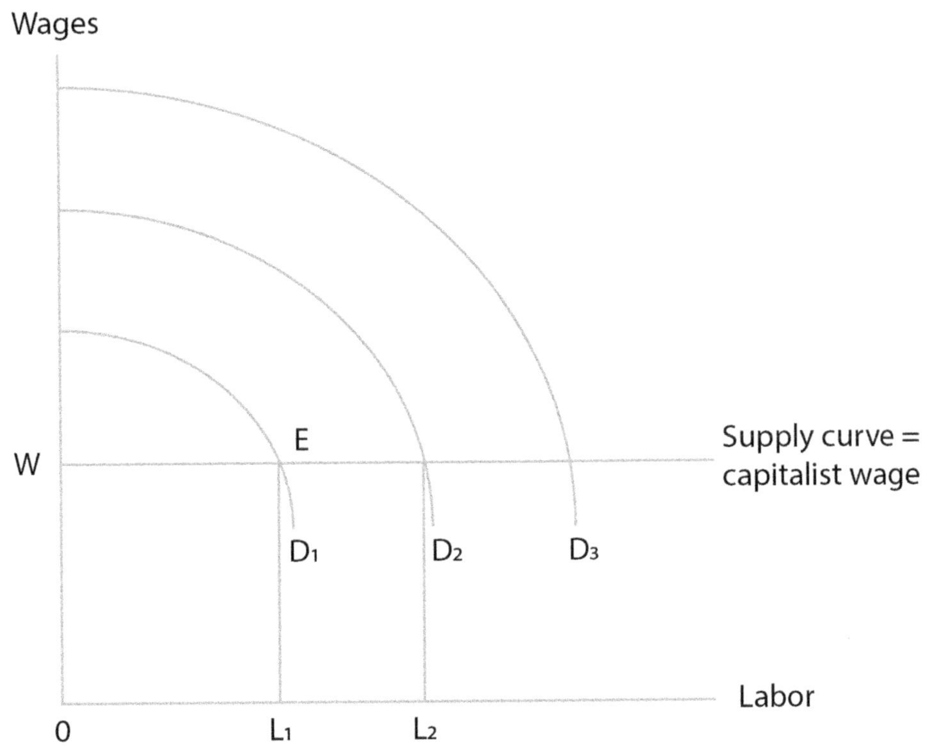

Image 4.1

Lewis assumes that most profits are saved and invested, and all wages are consumed. In the first period, the demand curve for labor is D_1 and the supply curve is infinite, so it is a horizontal line at the wage rate W. When demand equals supply, the market is in equilibrium and L_1 amount of labor is hired at the given wage W. The total amount of wages paid out is given by the rectangular area WEL_10, and the rest of the area under the demand curve and above the wage is profit, which is reinvested. In the second period, with more capital, the demand curve for labor moves out to D_2 and L_2 amount of labor is hired at the same wage W. More profits are made, and the demand curve moves out further, and the process continues. This model assumes that profits are the main source of growth and capital accumulation, and the economy undergoes a structural transformation from a primarily subsistence economy to a capitalist industrialized economy.

Invitation to reflect: Take a moment to reflect on how humans living in these countries might experience this model.

There are clearly many problems with both of these theories. Rostow assumes a linear process of development when we know that, in reality, development is seldom a linear process. Lewis's theory assumes that agricultural output in the subsistence sector and wages in the industrial sector remain constant. In reality, as labor moves out of the subsistence sector, the output of food will fall, which leads to higher food prices, and the capitalists will have to pay more wages, resulting in falling profits. There is also the problem of seasonal demand for labor in the subsistence sector and the problem of aggregate demand to consume the increasing output being produced.

Structuralist Theories

Structuralist theories view economic development as the transformation of the structure of production to meet changing demands and make more productive use of technology. The theory suggests that as an economy grows, the pattern of demand changes and the economy is constantly adjusting but is able to do so imperfectly. The transformation of production requires the reallocation of labor and capital to more productive uses. This allocation may not happen automatically or it may happen with a lag due to structural bottlenecks of various kinds. Therefore, structural analysis does not assume that each factor will always be allocated to its very best use by the market mechanism. It does not assume that factors of production can easily move from one sector to another due to lack of substitutability. The inflexibility of the economy is the main obstacle to economic development. The most common example is in the labor market where people earn different wages in different sectors. This analysis recognizes the removal of structural bottlenecks as a major source of economic growth. A second source of disequilibrium is the failure to reallocate resources efficiently so as to increase exports or replace imports. The tendency of import demand to rise faster than GNP per capita, lack of incentives for producers to enter new markets, and policies that favor import substitution instead of export promotion all contribute to a chronic balance of payments problem.

Structuralists emphasize structural constraints to growth. They argue that certain institutional forces perpetuate underdevelopment. Estonian economist Ragnar Nurkse (1953) came up with what he called the vicious circles of poverty.

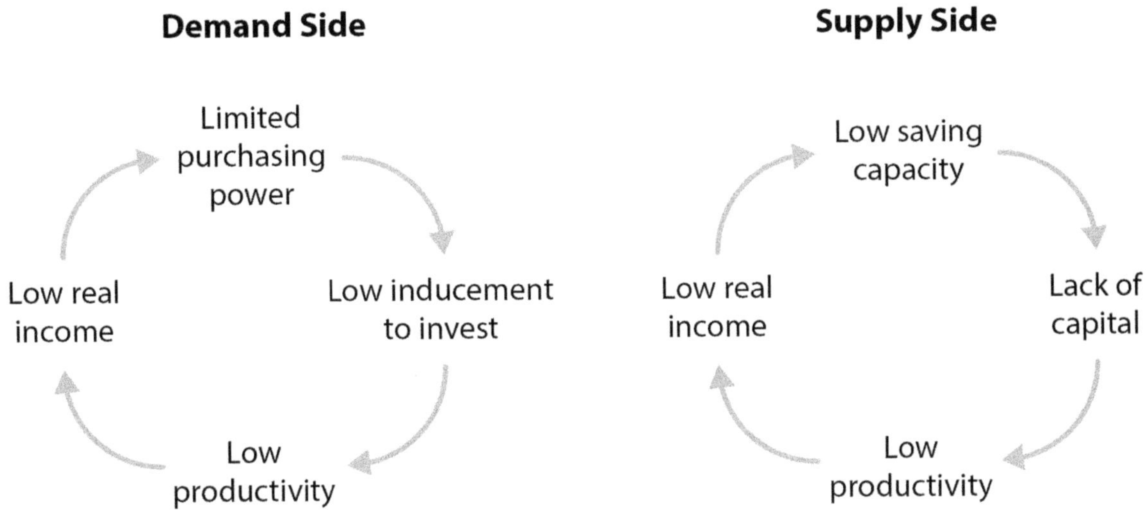

Image 4.2

It is argued that an injection of capital is needed to break the vicious circles. Often the capital comes from domestic capital formation urged by the government. These theories argued for strong government intervention in the market because the market is seen as being incapable of self-correction.

Neoclassical Theories (Neoliberal Policies)

The classical theories placed a lot of emphasis on capital accumulation and the role it plays in generating economic growth. The assumption is that labor is surplus in most developing countries and therefore the marginal product of labor is zero. **Neoclassical theories start with the assumption that all individuals are rational and maximize their own utility.** They also assume perfect competition in product and factor markets and the existence of infrastructure to support the smooth functioning of markets. Neoclassical analysis assumes that all factors of production add to total output. Wages and rents are measures of marginal factor productivities or contributions of factors of production to total output. GNP increases because of capital formation, labor force expansion, technological change, and the removal of market distortions. Shifts in resources from one sector to another will occur to bring the markets into equilibrium where all factors will produce equal marginal returns in all uses. Empirical evidence suggests that the contribution of capital has been the largest at well over 50% even in labor surplus countries. Empirical studies also found that a major portion of the increase in output remained unexplained as the residual, which includes improvement in the quality of labor, reallocation of resources to high productivity uses through the reduction of barriers, exploitation of economies of scale, and improved ways of combining things.

There is recognition that market failures can occur when any of the assumptions of perfect competition are not met, such as presence of monopolies, imperfect information, and externalities. But it is argued that government intervention cannot always resolve the matter or bring about a better outcome. The main focus or criteria used to measure better outcomes is economic growth and efficiency devoid of any concern for poverty or income distribution. This approach argues that the best policy is to remove all distortions to the market mechanism and to let the price mechanism provide the right incentives for resources to flow to their best use. "Get the prices right" is the policy implication in a nutshell.

Dependency Theories

The dependency school of thought is a strand of the structuralist paradigm. They argue that conditions of dependency in world markets of commodities, capital, and labor power are unequal and combine to transfer resources from dependent countries to dominant countries. According to this school of thought the problems of developing countries can only be understood in the context of their relationship to developed countries. The main idea is that developed countries are always the winners in any transaction with developing countries, whether in trade, investment, or technology. The underdevelopment of the periphery is a function of its external dependence on the center as affected by the operation of transnational capitalism. At the same time, historically development of the center happened at the expense of the periphery (colonization). According to this theory, the reason that this is a zero-sum game is because the dominant system is capitalism, and the driving force is the profit-seeking motive.

Dependency theory was seen as a major challenge to neoclassical theory. Dependency theorists saw external forces as the major problem of development, whereas neoclassical theorists saw internal forces as the major problem of development. Dependency theorists saw the relationship between the core and the periphery as an inherently unequal and exploitative relationship, whereas neoclassical theorists saw the relationship as an equal relationship. In the area of trade, the Singer-Prebisch thesis states that developing countries tend to export primary products that have very inelastic demand and supply curves. Over time substitutes to primary products are developed, which lowers the demand for primary products. In addition, most developed countries impose tariffs on primary products; therefore, the terms of trade move against developing countries. As a result, developing countries become worse off, and developed countries become better off. The more a country is dependent on primary products, the greater is the loss from trade. In addition, the trade terms for manufacturing goods improves over time; therefore, the gains from trade increase for developed countries.

According to dependency theory, foreign investment is aimed at removing the surplus from the periphery to the center by structuring the developed economy in an outward orientation that is characterized by the export of primary products, the imports of manufactures, and dependent industrialization. The high foreign exchange and import content of the kind of industrialization encouraged in these countries increases the demand for foreign exchange, which is the root cause of the dependence. Multinational corporations (MNCs) siphon off the surplus that would otherwise be used to finance domestic development and introduce economic and political distortions in the host country. MNCs introduce inappropriate capital-intensive technology that adds to the country's unemployment, increases inequalities of income, and alters consumer tastes, introducing consumerism that cannot be supported by the country's resources. MNCs also influence domestic policies to be in their favor to the detriment of the host country.

Invitation to reflect: Take a moment to reflect on when your life as a consumer or as a worker has been altered by MNCs in a way that was detrimental to you.

Gendering Theories of Development

The economic model being promoted clearly separated the economic sphere from the other spheres. The economic sphere was the privileged sphere because, according to this worldview, this was the sphere in which "productive activity" occurred, and if a country wanted to achieve rapid economic growth it needed to promote activities in this sphere. Importance was placed on exchange value versus use value. Different theories of development were articulated regarding how rapid economic growth could be achieved. Classical theories focused on the role of division of labor and international trade in bringing about rapid capital accumulation and economic growth. Rostow focused on the role of savings and investment, and Lewis focused on the importance of shifting labor from "unproductive" to "productive" sectors. While the structuralists emphasized the role of the government, the neoclassicists emphasized the role of the market, and the dependency theorists focused on the unequal power relationship between core and periphery countries, none of the theories questioned that economic growth was the ultimate goal. These theories led to different policies and strategies of development, which were promoted by the United States and Western Europe and organizations such as the World Bank and the International Monetary Fund. Although they might have worked in some cases, most of the time these policies did not work because they failed to take into account that the recipient countries might not have the same worldview (goals) as the "developed" countries. Secondly, even if they did, the institutional structure (economic, social, political, and cultural) in the recipient country might be very different from that of the United States and/or Western Europe.

Additionally, none of the theories specifically addresses gender issues, but each has had gendered impacts. American political scientist Catherine Scott (1995) reexamines theories of development from a gendered perspective by using the public/private dichotomy *object relations theory* and use of metaphors. Theories of development call for a greater separation between the public and the private spheres and place hierarchical value on the public sphere over the private sphere. For example, Rostow's theory assumes that productive activities occur only in the public sphere and envisions an economy that focuses on these high productivity sectors in order to enter the "takeoff stage" of development. By doing so, they privilege masculine skills/traits over feminine skills/traits. Women's association with the private sphere often leads to dependence on men and disenfranchisement. Dependency theory did not challenge the basic modern/traditional dichotomy set up by classical and neoclassical theories. Dependency theorists also maintain a public/private dichotomy in development policies. From their perspective, the public domain encompasses truly human activities where production goes beyond activities that are merely necessary to those that are creative. The private domain, which includes reproductive activities, is thought to consist of subsistence activities. Consequently, surplus is created primarily in the public domain, and conflict that results over the disposition of the surplus is a class conflict that occurs within the public domain. In this way, the private sphere and women are rendered invisible to the analysis. Dependency theorists never questioned the primacy of the public domain, nor did they question the need for modernization of the public domain for development to occur. They still saw industrialization and modernization as the ultimate goals of development. As much as dependency theorists believed that developing countries could not become developed if they continued to pursue a dependency relationship with developed countries, they also believed that developing countries wanted to and should eventually be like developed countries. In this way, they created a new dichotomy of core/periphery, which was based on the old modernization dichotomy of modern/traditional. Scott argues that these false binaries have been used by development agencies to exclude women from development initiatives and further exacerbate gender inequalities.

Scott also uses object relations theory to demonstrate how theories of development envision development as being a process of maturation where the economy has to break away from traditional ways of doing things and embrace modern ways and attitudes. This process is gendered because it sees the economy as being an infant that needs to establish its modernity (masculinity) by separating itself from the traditional (femininity) and becoming independent and forward thinking. For example, Lewis's theory requires countries to break away from the low productivity subsistence sector and focus attention on the high productivity modern industrial sector in order to achieve high rates of economic growth. In reality, the modern and the traditional coexist in most countries, and privileging one over the other often leads to failed development policies.

Scott demonstrates that development theorists often use gendered metaphors to characterize the development process. Classical theory requires the economy to "cut the bonds" to the economy of affection and requires a transition from a soft state to a hardened state. These gendered metaphors consistently devalue the traditional/soft/feminine qualities as requirements for modernity. Dependency theorists continue to use metaphorical language to depict how countries need to be independent and pull away from dependence if they are to become developed—in the same way that children need to pull away from their mothers to achieve maturity. Women are still subsumed as part of "nature," and hence their exploitation is seen as acceptable and unproblematic (similar to exploiting natural resources). As a result, dependency theory continued the masculinist nature of the development discourse. It failed to see that "productive labor" in the public sphere is impossible without "reproductive labor" in the private sphere, and this separation between the two spheres is a false dichotomy.

Structural Adjustment and the World Bank

The term structural adjustment refers to efforts by both the IMF and the World Bank to condition further lending to Third World governments on a series of reforms to increase economic growth, economic stability, and ameliorate balance of payments difficulties. Since the 1980s, more than 40 African countries have been required to adopt structural adjustment programs. The package includes reductions in public spending, reduced taxes on private business, deregulation, export promotion, devaluation of the currency, and welcome of foreign investment. The underlying theme is the supremacy of the market in achieving efficient allocation of resources. According to the World Bank and the IMF, governments have inhibited the proper functioning of the market, which is the chief reason for the country's underdevelopment. The role of government should be to promote private business and initiative and provide a framework to allow for the proper functioning of the price mechanism. The picture is drawn of a rational economic man impeded by the government, by tradition, and capable of innovation only under conditions of intense competition. In this view, achieving high rates of economic growth is a matter of having the right technology, organization, and policies to stimulate entrepreneurial activity. In many cases, these policies led to large-scale famine and instability. There is a neglect of institutional structures, communities, and households. In other words, the policies further widen the gap between private and public domain and end up ignoring women. Privatization, a major component of SA programs, also brings up the gendered question of who owns the property.

From WID to WAD to GAD

Broadly speaking, the field of gender and development starts with the recognition that the current structure is unjust and oppressive for women and that action is needed to liberate women from oppression. However, there are different theories about the fundamental cause for this oppression and the actions that are needed to correct it. Three of those theories are **Women in Development, Women and Development, and Gender and Development. We will examine each of these.**

WID (Women in Development): Gender issues first entered the development discourse in the 1970s. Danish economist, Ester Boserup (1970) was one of the first to demonstrate that economic development in the form of modernization of agriculture affected women very differently from men. Based on her examination of farming systems in Africa and South Asia, she argued that women played a significant role in food production but that the gender division of labor within agriculture was different across time and place. Up to that point, most development planners excluded women from the process since they assumed that women did not participate in agricultural work. They introduced technological innovations, such as the plow, but trained only men in these technologies. As a result, women were excluded and their participation in agricultural work was reduced to low productivity menial labor. The same process occurred in manufacturing industries, resulting in the defeminization of the labor force. Studies of historical and contemporary case studies reveal a similar pattern in countries across the world (Berik et al., 2008; Kucera & Tejani, 2014).

Boserup's work increased awareness within the United Nations and other development agencies of the women's role in economic development. Since then, the United Nations via its World Conferences on Women and the passage of the Convention on the Elimination of All Forms of Discrimination Against Women (CEDAW) in 1979 created growing awareness among policymakers and the larger global community that development is not complete until we achieve gender equality. CEDAW calls for gender equality in all laws from property to employment to marriage to reproductive rights. But it goes beyond legal equality by recommending temporary measures that might help correct past injustices, such as affirmative action or quotas. It also recommends family friendly policies that will allow men and women to participate in the labor force more equally. As of early 2022, 189 countries had ratified it. The remaining five include Islamic Republic of Iran, Somalia, Sudan, Palau, and the United States. The WID agenda not only led to the World Conferences on Women and the passage of CEDAW, but it also led to the creation of WID units in many countries and UN agencies.

Lobbying by women's groups has also forced the World Bank to address women, and the 1989 report discusses women 25 times, as compared to three times in the 1981 report. The Bank tried to address how to protect vulnerable groups from the effects of structural adjustment and the need to tailor structural adjustment policies to the circumstances of a particular country. They recognized that women are at a disadvantage because of their land rights, access to credit, technology, and education and are therefore ill-equipped to take advantage of better earnings opportunities. Their solution is that the state should enable women to participate in the public domain by removing obstacles in their way, while at the same time playing a minimal role and being neutral in incentives. The contradiction is that the Bank calls for greater incentive provided by the state for women and at the same time argues that the state is bad at picking winners. The Bank never challenges the notion that women are in the private domain, that they provide unpaid labor. Instead, they argue that time-saving devices should be introduced so that time is freed up for women to engage in income-generating activities. With less government spending, many activities move from the public to the private domain, increasing the burden for women rather than lessening them. The "women question" is then framed as a question of inclusion of women into the public arena where development happens—rather than a question of including the private sphere into the discussion.

Liberal feminists like Boserup and others believe that the development process largely ignored women, and women indeed need to have access to the benefits of development. They believe that the model of man the breadwinner–woman the homemaker is the problem. Prior to the 1970s, development planners assumed that women were largely homemakers and mothers and, therefore, did not include them in development initiatives that were focused on making the public sphere more productive. The WID approach argued for greater access for women to the public sphere via education, productive jobs, and family friendly policies. In other words, they did not challenge the development process itself, but they wanted to ensure that women were included and benefited from the process.

Scott (1995) examines how the "women question" plays out in the context of Angola and Mozambique. Both countries provide examples of revolutionary governments, which brought the possibility of change in conditions for women. While it is true that there were improved opportunities for women in terms of education, health, etc., the basic problem of the invisibility of the private sphere remained unquestioned. Women were encouraged to be "producers" and participate in the public sphere, but their labor in the private sphere remained unrecognized and this only meant that women were subject to more pressures than before. Often policies failed to take into account that women are constrained by their responsibilities in the private sphere. These policies also failed to question the power relationships within the household between men and women, and therefore the "women question" remained unaddressed.

WAD (Women and Development): Structural feminists believe that gender inequality needs to be placed in a much larger structural context (Elson & Pearson, 1981; Beneria & Sen, 1982). They argued that class struggle over surplus is at the center of analysis. Spanish American economist Lourdes Benería and Indian feminist scholar Gita Sen (1982) argued that oppression and exploitation are structurally maintained by systems of patriarchy and capital accumulation. It is not enough to look at gender inequality in isolation without also considering class exploitation. According to structural feminists, it is imperative for middle-class and upper-class women to acknowledge their role in exploiting their working-class brothers and sisters and stand in solidarity with them to improve their living and working conditions before they address the broader patriarchal forces that exploit and bind them together. To that end, Sen along with others founded Development Alternatives with Women for a New Era (DAWN) in 1985. The founders of DAWN argued that development policies must be created in collaboration with the poorest women in developing countries because they were the most disadvantaged. Development policies must make women better off on their own terms for the development process to be successful.

Invitation to reflect: Take a moment to reflect on a policy that might be different if we included the perspective of those who were the most disadvantaged group in society.

GAD (Gender and Development): Finally, with the rise of *postmodernism,* the GAD approach sought to bring these two strands together by reaffirming that gender is still the fundamental category of analysis, but that we need to situate it within the specific cultural, historical, social context within which women experience their lives. Postmodern and postcolonial feminist scholars remind us about the power of narratives and discourses about gender and race and urge us to question these limiting and often hegemonic views that can have such devastating consequences. The solution lies in recognizing the unique and specific needs of different groups of women, while rejecting all hierarchical relationships and structures of domination. This will allow for the liberation of men, women, and children from oppression. This approach focuses on policies that allow for full participation and expression for women and men in the development process.

Benería, et al. (2016) argues that there are three major barriers to achieving the goal of true gender equality:

- First, seeing gender equality as a means to an end versus an end in itself. Development planners have often used women to further goals, such as providing women with reproductive technologies to achieve population control goals versus for the empowerment of women. Often providing women access to education or jobs has been framed as an efficiency strategy, i.e., educated women make more productive workers or increased labor force participation by women will increase the GDP.
- Second, using solutions based on models that are ahistorical and apolitical. Planners have simply added women to existing models as though they were the missing ingredient, versus trying to understand the social, political, and historical context within which gender relations exist.
- Third, failing to see gender equality as part of a larger system of oppression based on race, class, gender, and other historically marginalized social identities. It is often less threatening to the status quo to see gender equality in isolation, versus as part of an intersectional and interconnected web of oppression. The capabilities and human rights approach make the case for gender equality by arguing that "all persons have the right to lead a dignified human life" and the goal of policies should be to try and provide all persons with the opportunities to pursue this life.

Role of Feminist Economics

Feminist economists took on the task of providing structural explanations for gender inequities and of seeking to move toward a world where gender inequities are eliminated. These contributions will be discussed in greater detail in later chapters. Although feminist scholarship has had a profound impact on many academic fields, mainstream neoclassical economics has continued to resist the challenge posed by many feminist economists. Mainstream economists in the United States started paying attention to the women's role in the economy in the 1950s and 1960s, when increasing numbers of middle-class women started entering the paid workforce at the same time that the average income of their husbands was increasing. Jacob Mincer, American neoclassical labor economist, argued that rising levels of education and incomes for women increased the opportunity cost of not entering the labor force (Mincer, 1962). He argued that while rising family incomes reduced the incentive to enter the labor force, higher opportunity cost increased the incentive to enter the labor force, i.e., the substitution effect is stronger than the income effect. Mainstream economists also started paying attention to the gender wage gap.

Nobel Prize winning American economist Gary Becker argued that differences in human capital explained much of the gender wage gap (Becker, 1964). Women chose majors and resulting jobs that paid less because they wanted the flexibility of taking care of their families and being able to participate in paid employment. Their discontinuous workplace attachment and lower investment in education and training resulted in lower wages. Becker's human capital model ascribed the gender pay gap to choices women made versus structural inequalities. He never questioned why certain kinds of jobs were valued more than others. He also never questioned why taking care of the family was solely the woman's responsibility. Becker also laid the groundwork for the new field of household economics, which applied principles of rational choice and individual utility maximization to the family. Becker (1981) used this model to justify the sexual division of labor within the household. He argued that men and women had different relative productivities in household activities and workforce activities. Men were assumed to be relatively more productive in workforce activities, and women were relatively more productive in household activities. As a result, men had a higher opportunity cost of wages foregone when they participated in household activities. According to Becker, both men and women would be better off, in terms of higher shared family output, if men specialized in workforce activities and women specialized in household activities.

Feminist economists strongly objected to the application of narrow assumptions of opportunity cost and utility maximization to the household. They argued that household activities are often rendered invisible and are not considered as valuable as workforce activities, and hence women who specialize in household activities experience a precarious dependence on men for access to market goods and services.

Feminist economists had to deconstruct the starting assumptions of standard economic theory, such as the assumption of the *rational economic man* who is an atomistic, ahistorical individual focused on maximizing his own self-interest. At the same time, Becker's model assumes that in the household human beings were benevolent and cooperative. Feminist economists have argued that human beings, both men and women, are much more complex and are capable of self-interested behavior. But they are also capable of empathy and collaboration, and moreover all of these behaviors are socially conditioned. Feminist economists focused on making gender the central category of analysis and social provisioning the chief activity under study (Benería et al., 2016). It is important to make visible the ways in which the unpaid/underpaid work of mostly women contributes to social provisioning and social reproduction. Ester Boserup (1970) focused on the unpaid work of women in subsistence farming. The study done by Indian economist Devaki Jain was one of the first to make visible the substantial amount of unpaid work done by women in India (Jain & Chand, 1982). American anthropologists June Nash and Helen Safa (1985) demonstrated how the extensive unpaid work of peasant women living in the Andes and factory workers in Brazil, Mexico, Jamaica, and Puerto Rico affected their paid employment.

It is also important to highlight gender inequalities in ownership of land and other assets. Land ownership can have a significant impact on the well-being of women and their children in terms of food security, physical safety, decision-making capabilities, and access to credit. Feminist economists have challenged Becker's theory of the family and the household as a harmonious unit. Amartya Sen's household model of cooperative conflict (1990) was a significant shift in the way that economists viewed the household. His theory provided a theoretical framework within which women's subordinate position could be better understood. Feminist economists have also challenged macroeconomic policies based on standard economic theory by considering the gendered impact of structural adjustment policies (SAPs) of the 1980s and 1990s. The austerity measures that were central to the SAPs led to a decline in public provisioning, which disproportionately affected women and children.

Additionally, feminist economics has converged with ecological economics with a shared concern for social provisioning for current and future generations. Women's work and the natural world are similarly exploited and undervalued, facilitating a convergence of interests and methodologies across the two fields.

Indian scholar and ecofeminist Vandana Shiva (1988) led the way in bridging the concerns of environmental activists and feminists to create a more unified and inclusive agenda. The impact of coalescing these interests can be seen in the sustainable development goals and the post-COVID feminist plan. While different groups of women have different agendas and issues that are more relevant for them, it is important that we support each other and work together to achieve our interdependent and interrelated goals. As Audre Lorde reminds us, it is not our differences that immobilize us but our silences.

Key Takeaways

Below are the key ideas to take away from this chapter:

- Concepts of gender and the associated concepts of masculinity and femininity are socially constructed and valued to create difference and hierarchy.
- Feminists are those who want to make the man–woman relationship one of equals. However feminism was initially based on the experiences of middle-class White feminists. As a result, women of color within the United States and around the world resisted and challenged the hegemonic representation of women of color as helpless, backward, and in need of saving by White women.
- Based on the definition of economic development as economic growth, mainstream economists provided different theories about how to achieve high economic growth. None of these theories questioned that economic growth is necessary for development. Additionally, none of them specifically address gender issues, but they have had gendered impacts.
- The field of gender and development starts with the recognition that the current structure is unjust and oppressive for women and that action is needed to liberate women from oppression. But there are different theories from WID to WAD to GAD about the fundamental cause for this oppression and the actions that are needed to correct it.
- Feminist economists took on the task of providing structural explanations for gender inequities and of seeking to move toward a world where gender inequities are eliminated. Feminist economists focused on making gender the central category of analysis and social provisioning the chief activity under study. They made visible the ways in which the unpaid/underpaid work of mostly women contribute to social provisioning and social reproduction.

Comprehension Questions

Directions: Use what you have learned in this chapter to help you respond to the questions below:

- How does the social construction of concepts of gender and the associated concepts of masculinity and femininity contribute to gender oppression?
- Mohanty and Abu-Lughod argue that Western feminists based on their own experiences and worldview constructed the concept of the "Third World woman" or the "Muslim woman." Discuss why this construction is problematic and contributes to gender oppression.
- Compare and contrast the classical and neoclassical theories of economic development.

- In what way does the dependency theory of development challenge the neoclassical theory of development?
- Compare and contrast the way in which Scott and Beneria discuss the gendered nature of the public/private dichotomy and its effects on outcomes for women.
- How did mainstream economists address gender issues in the labor market and in the household?
- How did feminist economists challenge the way mainstream economists address gender issues in the labor market and in the household?

References

Abu-Lughod, L. (2011). Do Muslim women really need saving? Anthropological reflections on cultural relativism and its others. In N. Visvanathan, L. Duggan, N. Wiegersma, & L. Nisonoff (Eds.), *The Women, Gender and Development Reader* (2nd ed., pp. 89–94). Zed Books.

Becker, G. (1964). *Human Capital: A Theoretical and Empirical Analysis, with Special Reference to Education.* National Bureau for Economic Research (pp. 16–187).

Becker, G. (1981). *A Treatise on the Family.* Harvard University Press.

hooks, b. (2015). Ain't I a Woman: Black Women and Feminism. New York: Routledge.

Benería, L. & Sen, G. (1982). Class and gender inequalities and women's role in economic development— theoretical and practical implications. *Feminist Studies,* 8(1), 157–78.

Benería, L., Berik, G., & Floro, M. (2016). *Gender, Development, and Globalization: Economics as if All People Mattered* (2nd ed.). Routledge.

Berik, G. (2008). Growth with gender inequity: Another look at East Asian development. In G. Berik, Y. van der Muelen Rodgers, & A. Zammit (Eds), *Social Justice and Gender Equality: Rethinking Development Strategies and Macroeconomic Policies* (pp. 154–86). Routledge.

Boserup, E. (1970) *Woman's Role in Economic Development.* New York: St. Martin's Press.

Elson, D. & Pearson, R. (1981). Nimble fingers make cheap workers: An analysis of women's employment in Third World export manufacturing. *Feminist Review,* 7(1), 87–107.

Jain, D. & Chand, M. (1982). Report on a time allocation study—its methodological implications. In Institute of Social Studies Trust: Technical Seminar on Women's Work and Employment, New Delhi.

Kishwar, M. & Vanita, R. (Eds.). (1984). *In Search of Answers: Indian Women's Voices from Manushi.* Zed Books.

Kucera, D. & Tejani, S. (2014). Feminization, defeminization and structural change in manufacturing. World Development, 64 (pp. 569–582).

Lewis, W. (1955). *The Theory of Economic Growth.* Homewood.

Mies, M. (1986). *Patriarchy and Accumulation on a World Scale.* Zed Books.

Mincer, J. (1962). Labor force participation of married women: A study of labor supply. In *Aspects of Labor Economics,* National Bureau for Economic Research (pp. 63–105). Princeton University Press.

Mohanty, C. (1991). Under Western eyes: Feminist scholarship and colonial discourses. In C. Mohanty, A. Russo, & L. Torres (Eds.), *Third World Women and Politics of Feminism* (pp. 51–80). Indiana University Press.

Nash, J. & Safa, H. (1985) *Women and Change in Latin America.* Bergin and Harvey Publishers.

Nurkse, R. (1953). *Problems of Capital Formation in Underdeveloped Countries.* Oxford: Basil Blackwell.

Oakley, A. (1972). *Sex, Gender and Society.* Harper & Row Publishers.

Oyewumi, O. (2002). Conceptualizing gender: The eurocentric foundations of feminist concepts and the challenge of African epistemologies. *Jenda: A Journal of Culture and African Women Studies,* 2(1).

Rostow, W. (1961). *The Stages of Economic Growth.* Cambridge.

Scott, C. (1995). *Gender and Development.* Boulder: Lynne Rienner Publishers.

Sen, A. (1990). Gender and cooperative conflicts. In I. Tinker (Ed.), *Persistent Inequalities: Women and World Development* (pp. 195–223). Oxford University Press.

Shiva, V. (1988). *Staying Alive: Women, Ecology and Development.* Zed Books.

Chapter 5

Patriarchy and Capital Accumulation

> We understand that women's oppression today is part and parcel of capitalist (or socialist) patriarchal production relations, of the paradigm of ever-increasing growth, of ever-increasing forces of production, of unlimited exploitation of nature, of unlimited production of commodities, ever-expanding markets and never-ending accumulation of dead capital.
>
> —Maria Mies (1986)

From Local Stories to Global Visions

The Indian Law Resource Center reports a rising epidemic of sexual violence against indigenous women. More than one in two American Indian and Alaska Native women has experienced sexual violence. On some reservations, indigenous women are murdered at more than 10 times the national average in the United States. More than 96% of these crimes are reportedly committed by those who are not American Indians, and the United States, until very recently, has severely limited the ability of American Indian nations to prosecute those who are not American Indians. Federal prosecutors who have the ability to prosecute these cases have declined to do so. On November 15, 2021, after years of advocacy work by the Indian Law Resource Center, Native women's organizations, and American Indian and Alaska Native nations, President Biden signed the Executive Order on Improving Public Safety and Criminal Justice for Native Americans and Addressing the Crisis of Missing or Murdered Indigenous People. Section 1 of the executive order states, *"Generations of Native Americans have experienced violence or mourned a missing or murdered family member or loved one, and the lasting impacts of such tragedies are felt throughout the country. ... Native American women, in particular, are disproportionately the victims of sexual and gender-based violence. ... And the vast majority of Native American survivors report being victimized by a non-Native American individual."*

Invitation to reflect: Take a moment to reflect on the layers of social injustice experienced by American Indian and Alaska Native women and their communities.

Introduction

Chapters 1, 2, and 3 provide a broadly accepted and shared understanding of the concepts of social justice, compassion, and development. In chapter 4 we focused our attention on the concepts of gender and feminisms. In chapter 5, we will analyze how patriarchy and capital accumulation have historically relied on each other to create and sustain systems of oppression based on gender, class, race, and national identity. We know that gender inequalities have existed for a very long time across the world. While the form it has taken has varied across time and space, we are left asking how and why the man–woman relationship became oppressive. In this chapter we will explore some of the answers to this question, while resisting the tendency to fall into traps of intellectual laziness and false equivalencies that will suggest that this situation is somehow "natural" or "meant to be" and therefore cannot be questioned or challenged. Systems of oppression are socially constructed and maintained by those who benefit from such a system and sometimes by those who don't benefit but have been socialized into believing that there are no other options. Our task in this chapter is to understand that systems of patriarchy and capital accumulation are not inevitable, but instead came about because of particular actions taken by human beings at particular moments in time. If we can understand how and why that came to be, then we can understand how to change this oppressive relationship into a relationship of equals where we recognize our interdependence with each other and with our environment and learn how to flourish together. We will also understand how gender oppression is connected to other systems of oppression, necessitating a coordinated dismantling of all oppressive systems.

How and Why Did the Male–Female Relationship Become Oppressive?

Let us start by defining the concept of patriarchy. **The word "patriarchy" literally means "rule of the father." It refers to a historical and socially constructed system of male dominance as a whole and male domination over women in particular.** According to Mies (1986), patriarchy is built upon socially constructed concepts of *labor* and *productivity.* Mies attempts to trace the social origins of the sexual division of labor and explains why and how this division of labor became an exploitative arrangement. Within this system, women giving birth to children and taking care of their children and their families is seen as being "natural." Mies characterizes this view in the following way: "All the labour that goes into the production of life, including the labour of giving birth to a child, is not seen as the conscious interaction of a human being *with n*ature, that is, a truly human activity, but rather as an activity *of n*ature, which produces plants and animals unconsciously and has no control over this process" (Mies, 1986, p. 45). Labor performed by the breasts or the womb is seen as being natural and therefore not productive labor. Viewing productive labor in this way allows the "natural" work done by women to be rendered invisible and appropriated by men and by capital. Thus, biological determinism has often been proffered as the explanation for why women are oppressed. According to this view, men are able to dominate over women because their work is more productive and more valuable. We are led to believe that men are "naturally" stronger and more productive and are able to provide for and protect women who are "naturally" weaker and less productive than men.

Invitation to reflect: Take a moment to reflect on when you might have been told that you were "naturally" stronger or weaker (or another trait) because of your gender. How did it make you feel? What if it isn't true? How would you feel then?

Instead, Mies and other feminists suggest that we define **productive labor as work that contributes to the production and flourishing of life.** Throughout human history, human beings have had needs, and we have had to figure out how to meet these needs. We have also needed to create other human beings. We have used our bodies to interact with our environment to meet the needs of our bodies. Human beings have also had the ability to reflect and make meaning of our existence and communicate that meaning to each other. Men and women experience their bodies differently, but the ways in which these differences are understood and evaluated is socially constructed within a particular historical and social context. In other words, our *history*—or as feminists have argued our *herstory*—*h*as always been socially constructed. Therefore, when we look back with a feminist lens at pre-patriarchal societies, we can see that women did in fact consciously and with reflection learn how to use their bodies to contribute to the production and flourishing of life. Studies have shown that women developed the knowledge and means to control the number of children they wanted to have (Fisher, 1979; Ehrenreich & English, 1973). The earliest methods of contraception relied on plants and herbs, and the knowledge was passed down from mother to daughter. Women also learned to use their bodies to sustain life through the milk she produced, but also the food she needed for her own daily sustenance, which led to foraging and gathering activities. The need for daily sustenance and the experience of interacting with plants led to the invention of settled cultivation in the Neolithic age, which scholars attribute to women (Childe, 1976). Women and children were probably the first social unit, and the food they produced/gathered/stored was the result of conscious, reflective, innovative, collaborative effort and planning to meet present and future needs. They developed the knowledge and tools—such as the hoe and the basket—to make the cultivation and storage of food possible (Reed, 1975; Thomson, 1965; Chattopadhyaya, 1973).

Challenging Man the Hunter and Protector Explanation

Recent findings from archeological excavations of 9,000-year-old burial sites from across the Americas challenge the man-the-hunter model by suggesting that female big-game hunters were fairly prevalent in early hunter–gatherer societies (Haas et al., 2020). Research has found that alloparenting, a practice wherein people other than parents provide childcare, would have allowed men and women to participate in hunting (Hrdy, 2009). Ecological conditions in some parts of the world may have necessitated more big-game hunting, which probably required participation by men and women to improve chances of success (Haas et al., 2020). Other studies have found that hunter–gatherer societies were more gender equal than agricultural societies (Iversen & Rosenbluth, 2010).

Feminist research has challenged in another way the man-the-provider model, labeling men as chief breadwinners and protectors of women (Martin & Voorhies, 1975; Goodale, 1971). Their research revealed that in many parts of the world, such as sub-Saharan Africa, gathering activities provided the majority of food for daily sustenance, whereas hunting provided the occasional meat (20% to 30%) because hunting activities were riskier and less stable. There is also evidence from coprolites revealing that 200,000 years ago the human diet was mostly vegetarian (Fisher, 1979). In other words, hunting contributions to calorie intake were sporadic, and the ability to hunt was based on women's ability to provide daily sustenance through gathering and foraging activities (Hunn, 2000). These studies suggest that men did not have an economic advantage over women, and therefore that cannot be the answer as to why the male–female relationship became an exploitative one. The answer must lie elsewhere.

Considering Development of Tools and Use of Violence Explanation

Mies suggests that the division of labor between men and women in societies where men were primarily the hunters and women were primarily the gatherers is characterized by the qualitatively different way men and women acted upon their environment. According to Mies, women's work as gatherers, nurturers, and cultivators was in harmony with their own bodies and their environment. Women were able to produce and grow food and create something new, whereas men's work as hunters was predatory and destructive. For men's work to be considered "productive" the use and development of certain kinds of tools were required. Using the man-the-hunter framework, Mies argues that the hunter model required men to develop tools that were capable of killing animals. Over time it became clear that these tools could and would be used against human beings. It is important to recognize that hunting weapons do not have to be used to exploit other human beings, but rather they create potential for exploitation. These tools could be used in a coercive way to appropriate and steal that which was produced by other human beings. The full potential of their control over the means of destruction became apparent with the domestication of animals and the domestication of women, who were relegated to the role of breeding children. Women became defined as part of nature—as part of the physical preconditions for patriarchal production. Women did not voluntarily agree to being oppressed and having their contributions appropriated by men. Men were able to maintain an exploitative relationship with women through the use and threat of violence.

As the mode of production changed from hunter–gatherer societies to pastoral nomads to agriculturalists, the theories about origins of patriarchy took different forms. Several studies suggest that the move to agricultural societies in the early Neolithic age heralded the origins of systematic gender inequality. They found that gender inequality was more likely to emerge in those parts of the world where early systems of agriculture depended on the use of ploughs (Iversen & Rosenbluth, 2010) and those that focused on cereal production (Hansen et al., 2015). The rise of feudalism heralded yet another spate of wars and more violence as new lands and peasants were acquired whose labor was now appropriated by the feudal lords. Women continued to be marginalized and their productive capacities diminished, their knowledge questioned and demonized through witch hunts and other acts of violence by the ruling class, the clergy, and later the state. Women were considered the property of their fathers and then their husbands. Feminist research has revealed that between the 14th and the 18th-century, millions of women were tortured, beaten, and burnt under the guise of witch hunts (Ehrenreich and English, 1973).

The following is an excerpt from a description of a witch trial held on October 31, 1724:

> Torture of Enneke Fristenares from Coesfeld (Munster): Then Dr Gogravius ordered the fifth degree: The accused was hung up and beaten with two rods—up to 30 strokes. She was so exhausted that she said she would confess, but with regard to the specific accusations she

continued to deny that she had committed any of the crimes. The executioner had to pull her up till her arms were twisted out of their joints. For six minutes this torture lasted. Then she was beaten up again, and again her thumbs were put into screws and her legs into the Spanish Boots. But the accused continued to deny that she had anything to do with the devil. As Dr Gogravius came to the conclusion that the torture had been correctly applied, according to the rules, and after the executioner stated the accused would not survive further torturing Dr Gogravius ordered the accused to be taken down and unbound. (quoted in Becker et al., 1977, 433–435, Trans. Mies)

Invitation to reflect: Take a moment to reflect on and imagine that Enneke, the accused woman, is your sister or mother or friend. How does that make you feel?

Millions more women had their property and jobs taken away, including autonomy over their bodies and reproductive capacities. Women resisted these attacks in various ways, including creating spaces for themselves to gather such as the Brethren of the Free Spirit, which was a sect that rejected the institution of marriage and embraced communal living and the equality of women's rights. Many members of this sect were later burnt as heretics (Cohn, 1970). With this analysis, Mies brings to the forefront issues of male violence and domination. Mies makes clear that this oppression is not inborn or biological. In other words, she does not want to reduce it to biological determinism. Men don't exploit women because it is inherently in their nature to do it, but because they have an incentive to do it. According to Mies, men exploited women in order to have control over the surplus and their access to tools of destruction and coercion gave them the means to do so. The witch trials are just one example of the extreme torture and burning of women to control their bodies, their productive capacities, and to set an example for other women who might resist the patriarchal system of oppression. Once the system of oppression is institutionalized and normalized, there is less need for direct physical violence because the system reinforces itself through a web of processes, norms, beliefs, and institutions.

Role of Capital Accumulation

We now analyze the role of capital accumulation in maintaining and perpetuating patriarchal systems of oppression. **Capital accumulation is a process of unlimited economic growth, ever increasing production of goods and services, and the capital needed to fuel this growth.** While technological change might allow us to produce more output with the same inputs, at some point this growth can only occur as a zero-sum game where one group of countries become *overdeveloped* at the expense of another group of countries that become increasingly *underdeveloped, i.e.*, the rich get richer as the poor get poorer. As discussed earlier, women's labor is socially constructed to be natural, inborn, and unconscious, whereas men's labor is seen as productive, creative, and rational. In a patriarchy/capitalist system men hold power and control over resources by this sexual division of labor. Men, in general, did the type of work that was considered to create a surplus, whereas women did the type of work that enabled men to go out and create a surplus. Therefore, capital accumulation cannot exist without patriarchy because the very nature of capital accumulation requires the growing creation of surplus and this surplus is not possible without the work women do in the private domain.

Structuralist Perspective

We will use a structuralist perspective to understand the relationship between capital accumulation and patriarchy. **A structuralist perspective broadly defined encompasses a worldview that society is in conflict and that these conflicts are rooted in class struggles and competition for power and scarce resources.** These theorists argue that domination and oppression are systemic and are structurally maintained. As part of this perspective, human beings are viewed as products of the ongoing interactive process of historical change. The specific mode of organizing labor in a given society determines the fundamental features of that society and the nature of its inhabitants. Human labor is seen as a means to an end until basic human needs are met and thereafter the development of human energy and creativity and the full and free expression of human potential is an end in itself. This potential is constrained by the labor necessary for survival, but also by class domination where even if the technology exists to meet basic needs for all, needs go unmet because power and wealth is concentrated in the hands of a few who exploit the labor of others for profit rather than the satisfaction of need.

According to Engels, the original division of labor was between man and woman for the propagation of children and based on nature. Women were concerned with reproduction of human life, and men provided the means of subsistence. Both contributions were seen as being vital and complementary so that both sexes enjoyed equal status. Changes in the relations of production and property rights led to the production of surplus and accumulation of wealth and men's control over this surplus and their need to pass it on to identifiable heirs. This led to the overthrow of mother's rights. Later, with industrialization and emergence of a market economy, the public/private sphere widened and women had less direct access to market resources, although there were differences between working-class women and women of the capitalist class. For the most part, class struggle plays a pivotal role in these theories, and, except for some passing references, the private domain is ignored, or worse, considered the unproductive sector of the economy. Italian feminist author Mariarosa Dalla Costa was one of the first to question the Engelian notion that women's work in the household was unproductive (Dalla Costa & James, 1975). She argues that the productive work of women in the household creates the preconditions for the productive work of men in the labor market. The creation of surplus starts with the unpaid work of women in the household. The exploitation of wage labor rests on the exploitation of nonwage labor.

Global Patriarchy Approach

Within the economic development literature, some feminists such as Mies, have used the basic structuralist perspective to develop a gendered reformulation of development. **They argue that capital accumulation is the driving force behind social conflict and that gender differences are systematically produced and maintained by the system of production and reproduction.** They placed gender conflict at the center of their theory and argued that the male–female relationship is fundamentally a relationship of power. Men as well as capital benefited from women's unpaid labor in the private domain. Mies superimposes the concept of patriarchy on the mode of production framework by arguing that male domination over women and nature was a far older system and that capitalism (and socialism) is just the recent manifestation of it. The patriarchal mode of production was a predatory one based on violence and the appropriation of surplus generated by the environment and by women. Once this predatory mode of production was established as the dominant paradigm, the deliberate development of technologies of warfare and transportation made it possible for Western Europe to conquer and pillage much of the rest of the world from the 15th century onward. With the rise of capitalism, the control over surplus accelerated as the ruling class was defined by owners of capital versus owners of land. Large-scale movement of peasants from the farm to the factory led to the creation of wage labor. At the same time, the ever-growing need for labor and raw materials led to violent colonization and enslavement of men, women, and children from large parts of Africa, Asia, and Latin America.

Mies analyzes the history of the related processes of colonization and *housewifization* and its current manifestation in terms of the new international division of labor. According to Mies, capitalism grew first with the exploitation of women and men in the laboring classes in Western Europe. When the limit had been reached in terms of fear of social unrest, limited availability of land, limited raw materials, and limited size of markets, exploitation moved to the colonies. This process was unpeaceful and accompanied by large-scale violence and extermination of large groups of people. The colonies, which were mostly inhabited by people of color, were seen as part of nature or savage (not quite human) and therefore exploitable by the "civilized" Europeans who were mostly white.

Over the last few centuries, racism and patriarchy worked together to create unprecedented capital accumulation and unprecedented violence. Several studies have revealed the inhuman treatment of men, women, and children by European trading companies and slave owners. Studies from the Caribbean have revealed that enslaved men and women were often forced to 20-hour days out in the field (Knight, 1970). Another study from Brazil revealed that planters would work their enslaved men and women so hard that they wouldn't survive beyond a year, but during that time they had managed to get enough work out of them to make it a worthy investment in their profit-driven calculus of human lives (Hall, 1971).

Invitation to reflect: Take a moment to reflect on and imagine that the slave owner is your brother or father or friend. How does that make you feel?

Colonies were seen as a source of raw materials, slave labor, and captive markets for sale of finished products. Rapid capital accumulation and economic growth in Western Europe was made possible by colonization. Goods were cheaply available for consumers in Western Europe because of slave labor. Trinidadian scholar and activist Rhoda Reddock's research on enslaved women in the Caribbean revealed that the concept of the housewife did not exist among slaves (Reddock, 1985). Women in the colonies were either considered part of the labor force to be exploited or breeders of future generations of slaves, depending on which representation was more cost effective to the colonizers. According to Jamaican sociologist Orlando Patterson (1967), the advent of large-scale sugar plantations led to a much greater demand for slave labor. It became cheaper to import slaves than to reproduce them so a strong anti-natalist policy was adopted.

Francisco d'Arango y Perreneo, the father of the slave plantation system in Cuba, is quoted as saying, "During and after pregnancy, the slave is useless for several months, and her nourishment should be more abundant and better chosen. This loss of work and added expense comes out of the master's pocket. It is he who pays for the often ineffective and always lengthy care of the newborn. This expense is so considerable that the negro born on the plantation costs more when he is in condition to work than another of the same age bought at the public market would have cost" (quoted in Hall, 1971, p. 24).

At other times, it became costly to import slaves and a pronatalist policy was adopted. Attempts were made to introduce the concept of marriage and the nuclear family among slaves in an effort to raise the fertility rate. There were various forms of resistance to these policies, especially from women who often ended their pregnancies rather than see their children become slaves. They did not see any benefit to marriage. They did not want to be beaten by their husbands in addition to being beaten by slave owners. Many slave owners viewed this equality between men and women as "primitive" and wanted to "civilize" the slaves into accepting so-called Christian values of female domestication and male domination.

At the same time that women in the colonies were being seen as labor, women in Europe were being domesticated and ideologically manipulated into thinking that motherhood and wifehood was their "natural" vocation. At the same time that labor in the colonies was being exploited, labor in Europe was being pacified by higher wages. Women were being asked to remain at home to raise children. This was the time that the nuclear family was introduced in Europe, where the man was defined as the breadwinner and the woman was defined as the housewife.

Invitation to reflect: Take a moment to reflect on the concepts of husband and wife. What images come to mind when you think of these words. How and when did you make these associations?

This model became popular around the early 19th century among the propertied classes. The poor were not considered worthy to have a "family." Only later in the 19th century did the nuclear family spread to all sections of the population. With the rise of capitalism, men became the ones to enter the labor force (public domain), and women were in charge of the household (private domain). This distinction between the public and the private domain widened with the spread of capitalism. There was a need to domesticate proletariat women and make them breeders of the labor force rather than members of the labor force. The housewife was also an agent of consumption. In addition, the housewife provided many services that were unpaid but were required for the maintenance of "productive" labor. The state, by giving full rights to the man as breadwinner, gave the man his own colony to exploit.

New International Division of Labor

With many colonies achieving independence by the mid-20th century, colonies were no longer a source of economic growth, and a new era of exploitation was established. Many labor-intensive industries moved to the "underdeveloped" countries to take advantage of the low-wage labor in these countries. As a result, there was increasing unemployment in the "overdeveloped" countries. Women in these countries were being thrown out of the formal sector and told to stay home and consume products produced in the "underdeveloped" countries. "Underdeveloped" countries increasingly produced for the consumption of the "overdeveloped" countries, instead of their own consumption. The cheap labor ensured that these goods could be sold at a cheaper price, thereby reducing social unrest. It has been found that most of the time when corporations move to "underdeveloped" countries in search of cheap labor, they hire women who work mostly in the unorganized, nonunionized sector and have fewer options. Because are often defined as housewives their income is seen as "supplemental." All these factors made it possible to pay women less.

At the same time, the World Bank and other international agencies were seeing this as a positive way of integrating women into development by bringing women into the public domain. This strategy involved giving women income-generating activities, which usually meant encouraging them to produce goods for export consumption rather than encouraging them to produce for themselves and for their children. Women in the "underdeveloped" countries were being seen as labor to be exploited, rather than as consumers or as breeders. In fact, population growth is seen as an obstacle to development, and women are in many instances (e.g., China) being forcibly asked to reduce fertility. This is the story of how patriarchy and the drive for capital accumulation created and perpetuated the oppressive male–female relationship.

Social Relations of Gender Approach

Another important contribution toward understanding how unequal gender relations are maintained and perpetuated was made by the social relations of gender feminists. **This group of feminists argue that although women and men are products of the structure and mode of production they operate within, they are still capable of coping with and seeking to transform the conditions of their lives.** While they agree that male domination may be a nearly universal phenomenon, it operates in more concealed and variable ways. Power in this analysis does not always operate through violence and force, but also through social relations that allow men to mobilize a greater range of resources in a greater range of institutional domains. They argued that seeing women as the primary category meant that the problem and the solution could be confined to women. They argued that while asymmetric gender relations arose in the domestic arena, they were reconstituted in the broader economic arena. The social rules and practices through which gender relations are constructed constitute a highly selective interpretation of biological differences where similarities are suppressed and differences exacerbated to ensure that the male and female of the species are channeled into oppositional categories of men and women.

Other social relations also mediate gender relations, such as class or race or kinship. In precapitalist societies, kinship organized social, economic, cultural, and political activities, and the domestic domain was the primary site of gender relations. In capitalist market-based societies where the public and private are more separate, the private domain remains the site of gender relations, but has implications for the apparently separate public sphere as well. The rules and practices of marriage, procreation, inheritance, and parenting all combine to ensure that in much of the world, women are responsible for care and nurture of the family and men are responsible for providing subsistence. However, the rules and practices through which familial relations are constructed and the scope they give women to change, adapt, and negotiate are endlessly variable. Therefore, it is argued that the social relations of gender approach will give a far better understanding of these differences than a model of global patriarchy can provide.

While the drive for capital accumulation imposes a specific logic on the possibilities open to different individuals, the diverse ways in which people organize their working and family lives change the impact capitalism has on different societies. In addition, different regimes of accumulation and different mechanisms of exploitation give rise to different outcomes for gender subordination. Beneria and Sen (1982) offer a number of examples where in some parts of sub-Saharan Africa with the commercialization of land, poor peasant families have lost land rights and common pool resources and women had to intensify their labor searching for fuel, carrying water, and processing food. This has been worse in those cases where men have gone to the cities in search of work, leaving subsistence production entirely to women. In urban Latin America, the entry of commercial capital has displaced women as independent artisans. In Southeast Asia, the setting of global market factories has led to increased use of women in urban areas as wage labor.

We can also find examples of unique family structures and social relations that perhaps challenge the dominant paradigm. One such example is found among the Mosuo community, who live in a remote province in Yunnan, China. One of the few existing matrilineal societies in the world, the Mosuo people trace their lineage down the mother's line. They don't have the institution of marriage or the nuclear family. Instead, the family includes the mother, her siblings, and her children. Men and women share a bond based on love, and they don't share the same family or home. Men live with their mothers, siblings, and their sisters' children. Women are the head of the household and have much more autonomy over their life decisions. Weaving is both a cultural skill and a way for women to provide for their families. In 2017, the Mosuo women made a deal with a department store in Singapore to sell their beautiful handwoven scarves as part of a United Nations Development Programme (UNDP) initiative.

Invitation to reflect: Take a moment to reflect on and imagine what it might be like to be part of the Mosuo community.

Domestic Mode of Production Approach

This theory tries to understand why the domestic sphere is rendered invisible by both neoclassicists and Marxists. **According to this theory, domestic work has remained invisible because its products are not priced and traded in the public arena.** The problem lies with the conception of production. The process of production can be seen as a continuous process, beginning with extraction of raw materials to their final human use. The convention among economists is to draw the line in the marketplace when the product is transferred to the final consumer, who does not return to the market for further resale. According to this theory, this convention is based on the notion of the capitalist mode of production. Any processing that happens outside of the capitalist mode of production is not considered significant because it is assumed that economic activity in the public domain is production and economic activity in the private domain is consumption.

In a modern capitalist economy, such a definition causes problems, but in a "developing" country the problem is worse. This theory argues that instead we should draw the line between production and consumption after the last activity that added more use value to the product than it consumed and before the first activity that consumed more value than it added. Let us consider an example of a chicken egg. It is a natural food, but it takes the work of many to get it from the hen to its consumer. According to the standard definition, production ended when the last wage worker checked it out at the grocery store or in the market. But using the second definition, more use value was added after buying it in the market. It must be taken home, stored in the fridge, taken out at a later date, and cooked. Once ready to eat, it must be served, which may involve more processing for children than others. All of this involves work and certainly adds use value to it and should therefore be considered production.

The second idea is the difference between production and reproduction developed in Marxist thinking that production *adds* use value and reproduction *maintains* use value. If value is placed only on adding use value, then activities that maintain use value which also require labor are ignored. In Marxist tradition, the working class of the domestic mode of production tends to be women and the controlling class that has control over the surplus tends to be men. It is an exploitative mode of production because all production is done almost exclusively by women and the product is consumed by heads of households who tend to be men. The reasons that women remain in this mode of production are low bargaining power resulting from lack of access to ownership of their own means of domestic production. This could be achieved by legal, ideological, social, political means, or compulsion and violence.

Constructing Alternative Visions from Lessons Learned

The answers we have unearthed to the question how and when did the male–female relationship become oppressive have taught us that men exploited women to appropriate the surplus generated by women and women are also exploited by capital in their role as housewives and in their role as wage labor. We have also learned that violence was used to initiate and perpetuate oppression. From these lessons, we want to construct alternative visions based on the advice of Audre Lorde in a lecture given at a feminist conference at New York University in 1979 (Lorde, 2007):

> For the master's tools will never dismantle the master's house. They may allow us temporarily to beat him at his own game, but they will never enable us to bring about genuine change. And this fact is only threatening to those women who still define the master's house as their only source of support.

As feminists, we choose not to replace one form of hierarchy with another. We intentionally and thoughtfully choose not to use violence and tools of oppression to advance our agenda. Instead, we seek to create a world with no hierarchies, where no one is exploited or oppressed. We choose compassion and the wisdom of our lived experiences to dismantle oppressive systems. We can start that process by first looking inward and asking ourselves when and in what situations we are the oppressor and when and in what situations we are the oppressed. Secondly, we can share our experiences with our fellow sisters and brothers and stand together against oppression in all its forms. This inner work must occur hand in hand with the work of forming alliances and building solidarity across differences. The compassionate approach demands that everyone is included and everyone belongs. It also demands that we do this work out of love, not hate.

Over the years I have shared with my dear beloved my experiences of growing up in India as a woman and then being here in the United States. He listens and asks me what I need from him to feel supported and heard. He shares with me his experience of being a Black man in America and how his ancestors did not have the luxury of packing a suitcase and choosing to come to the United States. And I listen and try to hold his suffering in my heart without bursting with anger and outrage at the enormity of his oppression. Instead, I am in awe of the courage that it took for him to defy all odds and become a first-generation university professor. I listen to the experiences of my American Indian friends, my Latina friends, my Jewish and Muslim friends, and my lesbian friends, and I recognize that my human heart has the capacity to expand and hold them all in compassion and action. There is much to celebrate in their achievements and much to struggle against in their suffering.

Invitation to reflect: Take a moment to reflect on how you can choose to not oppress and how you can stand up against being oppressed.

Key Takeaways

Below are the key ideas to take away from this chapter:

- Feminist research has challenged the man-the-provider model that men were the chief breadwinners and protectors of women. Instead, the research revealed that in hunter–gatherer societies women provided the majority of food for daily sustenance, whereas men provided the occasional meat from their hunting activities.
- Going back to hunter–gatherer societies, Mies explains that the male–female relationship became an exploitative one because men wanted to have control over the surplus that women generated and their access to tools of destruction and coercion gave them the means to do so.
- Mies superimposes the concept of patriarchy on the mode of production framework by arguing that male domination over women and nature was a far older system and that capitalism (and socialism) is just the recent manifestation of it.
- The patriarchal mode of production was a predatory one based on violence and the appropriation of surplus generated by the environment and by women. Once this predatory mode of production was established as the dominant paradigm, the deliberate development of technologies of warfare and transportation made it possible for Western Europe to conquer and pillage much of the rest of the world from the 15th century onward.
- Capital accumulation grew first with the exploitation of women and men in the laboring classes in Western Europe. When the limit had been reached, exploitation moved to the colonies. This process was accompanied by large-scale violence and extermination of large groups of people.
- At the same time that women in the colonies were being seen as slave labor, women in Europe were being domesticated and ideologically manipulated into thinking that motherhood and wifehood was their "natural" vocation.
- As feminists we seek to create a world with no hierarchies, where no one is exploited or oppressed. We choose compassion and the wisdom of our lived experiences to dismantle oppressive systems.

Comprehension Questions

Directions: Use what you have learned in this chapter to help you respond to the questions below.

- How and why did the male–female relationship become oppressive?
- How do patriarchy and capital accumulation work together to create and sustain systems of oppression based on gender, class, and race?
- How do the processes of colonization and housewifization work together to create and sustain systems of oppression based on gender, class, and race?
- How do social relations of gender perpetuate unequal gender relations?
- How does the definition of production and consumption explain unequal gender relations?
- What role does compassion play in the feminist construction of alternative visions?

References

Becker, B., Bovenschen, S., & Brackert, H. (1977). *Aus der Zeitder Verzweiflung: Zur Genese und Aktualitdt des Hexenbildes*. Frankfurt.

Benería, L. & Sen, G. (1982). Class and gender inequalities and women's role in economic development—Theoretical and practical implications. *Feminist Studies,* 8(1), 157–78.

Chattopadhyaya, D. (1973). *A Study in Ancient Indian Materialism, 3rd ed.* People's Publishing House.

Childe, G. (1976). *What Happened in History*. Penguin Books.

Cohn, N. (1970). *The Pursuit of the Millennium*. Paladin.

Dalla Costa, M. & James, S. (1975). *The Power of Women and The Subversion of the Community*. Falling Wall Press Limited.

Dyble, M., Salali, G., Chaudhary, N., Page, A., Smith, D., Thompson, J., Vinicius, L., Mace, R., & Migliano, A. Sex equality can explain the unique social structure of hunter-gatherer bands. *Science* 348, 796–798 (2015).

Ehrenreich, B. & English. D. (1973). *Witches, Midwives and Nurses: A History of Women Healers*. Feminist Press.

Fisher, E. (1979). *Woman's Creation*. Anchor Press.

Goodale, J. (1971). *Tiwi Wives*. University of Washington Press.

Haas, R., Watson, J., Buonasera, T., Southon, J., Chen, J. C., Noe, S., Smith, K., Llave, C. V., Eerkens, J., & Parker, G. (2020). Female hunters of the early Americas. *Science Advances*, 6(45), 1–10.

Hall, G. (1971). *Social Control in Slave Plantation Societies*. Johns Hopkins Press.

Hansen, C., Jensen, P., & Skovsgaard, C. (2015). Modern gender roles and agricultural history: the Neolithic inheritance. *Journal of Economic Growth*, 20(4), 365–404.

Hrdy, S. (2009). Mothers and Others: *The Evolutionary Origins of Mutual Understanding*. Harvard University Press, Cambridge.

Hunn, E. (2000). On the relative contribution of mean women to subsistence among the hunter–gatherers of the Colombia Plateau. In P. Minnis (Ed.), *Ethnobotany*: A Reader. Norman: University of Oklahoma.

Iversen, T., & Rosenbluth, F. (2010). Women, Work, and Politics: *The Political Economy of Gender Inequality*. New Haven, CT: Yale University Press.

Knight, F. (1970). *Slave Society in Cuba During the Nineteenth Century*. University of Wisconsin Press.

Lorde, A. (2007). The master's tools will never dismantle the master's house. Sister Outsider: Essays and Speeches, p. 110–114. Berkeley, CA: Crossing Press.

Martin, M. & Voorhies, B. (1975). *Female of the Species*. Columbia University Press.

Mies, M. (1986). *Patriarchy and Accumulation on a World Scale*. Zed Books.

Patterson, O. (1967). *The Sociology of Slavery*. Fairleigh Dickenson University Press.

Reddock, R. (1985). Women and slavery in the Caribbean: A feminist perspective. *Latin American Perspectives*, 12(1), pp. 63–80.

Reed, E. (1975). *Woman's Evolution from Matriarchal Clan to Patriarchal Family*. Pathfinder Press.

Thomson, G. (1965). *Studies in Ancient Greek Society: The Prehistoric Aegean*. Citadel Press.

Chapter 6

Women and the Global Economy: Current Trends

> Women's bodies and labor are used to consolidate global dreams, desires, and ideologies of success and the good life in unprecedented ways.
>
> —Chandra Talpade Mohanty, 2003

From Local Stories to Global Visions

Lourdes Lujan and Carmen Duran, two women working in the maquiladoras in Mexico assembling television sets, tell us their story in their own words in an award-winning documentary titled *Maquilapolis: City of Factories* (2006). They tell us that initially they appreciated the opportunity to earn $6 a day, which was more than they earned in other jobs. They used their incomes to support their families and make improvements in their sparse living conditions. But as time went on, they noticed that there were clear violations of labor standards as they were asked to work long hours without breaks, in toxic environments. When the women asked for better working conditions, the multinational companies closed shop and moved their factories to other countries, leaving these women without the promised severance pay. These factories also polluted the water around the area where they were located, which led to serious health complications for these women and their families. When they sought redress, they were denied, threatened, and terrorized in an effort to silence them. We invited some of these women *promotoras* to our campus (California State University, San Marcos) to talk to our students. They told us that despite all odds they continued to educate themselves and other workers of their rights and pursue legal action against the multinational corporation who had denied them their rights. They eventually won their case for severance pay. They also worked with environmental advocacy groups to pressure the Mexican government to enforce water pollution mitigation measures. We gave them a standing ovation as we clapped and cried with them, inspired by their courage and persistence.

Invitation to reflect: Take a moment to reflect on the layers of social injustice experienced by these women in Mexico as they struggled to feed their families and fight for their rights.

Introduction

In chapter 5, we discussed how patriarchy and capital accumulation have historically relied on each other to create and sustain systems of oppression based on gender, class, race, and national identity. In this chapter, we discuss the ways in which these systems of oppression continue to manifest themselves in the economic lives of women, men, and children in the labor market and in the household today. In particular, we will discuss the ways in which the global financial crisis of 2008 and the global public health crisis (COVID-19 pandemic) have exacerbated economic inequalities between men and women in the labor market and in the household.

Intensification of Global Economic Integration

During the last 50 years, we have experienced an unprecedented intensification of global economic integration in the form of expanded flows of trade, capital, finance, and labor across borders. This was made possible by the lowering of trade barriers, technological changes, and expansion of markets. It has given rise to global supply chains of increasing complexity and interdependence where different parts of the production process are occurring in different countries. It has changed the way we offer services and the way we travel across borders. It has brought me, along with countless others, to the United States to pursue graduate studies. It has also led to multiple global financial crises, the latest of which occurred in 2008, which started in one part of the world and then quickly spread to other countries due to increased global integration and lack of regulation of financial markets. It also led to the global pandemic that started in 2019 and quickly spread across the world.

During the last 70 years, there has been a concerted effort through a series of multilateral and bilateral negotiations to lower trade barriers and expand world trade. As a result, exports are almost 25% of global GDP today as compared to around 7% in 1948. There have also been regional shifts during this time with North America's share of world trade decreasing from 28.1% to 12.6% and Asia's share of world trade increasing from 14% to 34.3%. Much of this shift is caused by China's share of world trade increasing from 0.9% to 14.3%. There has been a similar increase in global capital flows. For example, the value of foreign direct investment globally increased from $12.4 billion in 1970 to $1.5 trillion in 2019. By comparison, the increase in global labor flows has been much smaller from 71 million in 1960 to 243 million in 2015.

Invitation to reflect: Pick an item that you have with you (a watch, a phone, a pen) and look at it like you are looking at it for the first time, reflecting on the process by which it may have been produced, assembled, and eventually used by you. Think about all the people who played a role in making that happen, feeling some gratitude toward them and feeling your connection with them. Would you still purchase this item if you knew the working conditions of the people who made it?

Rising Inequality

One of the major consequences of expansion of markets has been growing inequalities wherein some have prospered but the majority have experienced greater insecurity and environmental degradation. According to the World Social Report (2020), income inequality between countries has decreased in relative terms (largely due to economic growth in China) but has increased in absolute terms. The gap in mean per capita income between high and low-income countries increased from $27,600 in 1990 to over $42,800 in 2018. Income inequality has grown within most high-income countries around the world. About 27% of all income growth between 1980 and 2016 was captured by the global top 1% such that their share of income increased from 16% to 20% during this time period. By contrast, the share of the bottom 50% remained stagnant at 9%, exacerbating income inequalities within countries. The regional composition of the bottom 10% has changed substantially from 1988, when 40% of the bottom 10% lived in China (Lakner & Milanović, 2016) to 2008, when almost all people in this group lived in sub-Saharan Africa and India. Inequality within China increased during the 1990s and then decreased since 2008. Turning to wealth inequality, we find that the bottom 50% of the global population owned less than 1% of all wealth in 2018, whereas the top 10% owned 85% of all wealth and the top 1% alone held almost half of it (Shorrocks et al., 2018). Our ability to deal with crises is made far more difficult when we do so under conditions of extreme inequality.

Invitation to reflect: Take a moment to reflect on when you first became aware of your economic class. How did it make you feel?

The growing privatization of land and capital has concentrated assets in the hands of corporate entities (McMichael, 2012). Free markets are designed to spur competition and pick winners. If you have ever played the board game Monopoly, you know that even when everyone starts with the same initial endowment and is subject to the same rules, we still inevitably end up with one winner who takes all and many losers who are left with nothing. When you consider that in the real world, the starting point is never a level playing field and the rules do not apply to everyone in the same way, the process of increasing inequality is accelerated even further. People who have historically been marginalized, enslaved, and oppressed fall further and further behind. Growing political power of corporate entities has resulted in lowering of corporate taxes, and the resulting decrease in government revenue has led to a contraction in education, health, and social safety net programs (Lopez & Miller, 2008). Austerity policies implemented in response to the 2008 crisis had a similar effect (Peet, 2011). Therefore, those who lose from this process have no safety net to fall back on, and their life chances are further diminished with each crisis and each passing generation.

Rapid technological change has also exacerbated inequalities as some jobs are rendered obsolete and new jobs are created. Skilled workers are usually more able to take advantage of the new technologies and tend to benefit more than lower skilled workers, further increasing wage inequality. In addition, the digital divide, where 87% of those in high-income countries have internet access as compared to 19% in low-income countries, continues to persist, making it harder to access new opportunities. According to the Alliance for Affordable Internet (2021), globally men are 21% more likely to be online as compared to women, but these numbers hide huge regional differences. For example, the gender gap in internet use is 1% in North America (men's use is 95% and women's use is 94%), but the gender gap in internet use is 137% in South Asia (men's use is 37% and women's use is 18%). In the United States, the digital divide is primarily along racial and income lines. When we had to shut down in-person classes at our university in March 2020 and pivot to virtual instruction, we had to face the reality that many of our students, especially students of color from low-income households, did not have reliable access to the internet or to computers. We decided to hand out computers and hot spots to students to ensure that they could continue their education. But many parts of the world did not have access to resources, and students experienced a huge loss in learning during this time.

Climate change has also led to rising inequality as the impact of environmental degradation has disproportionately fallen on the poorest of the poor. Most of the poor live in tropical regions, and their livelihoods are often most directly dependent on environmental conditions. They are also the least able to shield themselves from environmental disasters and extreme weather patterns. It has been estimated that the ratio between the incomes of the richest 10% and the poorest 10% of the global population is 25% higher than it would have been without climate change (Diffenbaugh & Burke, 2019). Women have been particularly vulnerable to these changes, given that they are often the ones responsible for providing food and water for their families. If left unchecked, these changes will lead to rising numbers of women and their children facing extreme poverty and starvation in the next few years.

Invitation to reflect: Take a moment to reflect on extreme weather conditions and environmental degradation that you have experienced in the last few years. Did you and your community have the capacity to deal with it?

In addition, increasing numbers of poor men and women are participating in the unstable financial market as borrowers and lenders, which make them more vulnerable to the whims of financial markets and leads to greater inequality. Global flows of capital have increased female labor force participation in export-oriented jobs, but much of this labor is informal, performed under poor working conditions, and subject to the ebb and flow of global capital. While it has led to increased autonomy in some cases, there are many instances of increased exposure to violence, sexual abuse, and discrimination.

World of Paid Work

Over the last 50 years, more and more women have been incorporated into wage employment in agriculture, export-oriented manufacturing, and services. It has been accompanied by a trend toward growing informalization of the female labor market. The informal labor market has grown dramatically over the last couple of decades, and a majority of workers in the informal labor market are women. **The informal economy is characterized by poor working conditions, lack of regulation, low wages, and lack of labor contracts with health and other benefits.** Global corporations search for cheap labor, and in most countries women are the lowest paid segment of the labor market. Therefore, they tend to hire mostly women at very low wages. They are able to do so because in most cases women have very few alternatives. Women are often characterized as housewives with their income seen as being supplemental even though in many cases women are the primary wage earners in the family. Given women's responsibilities in the private domain, they often opt for flexible work conditions, which typically pay less than other jobs. This is especially true in the case of home-based workers where traditional gender roles are not challenged and women are not seen as wage workers even though they might be producing goods for export markets. In fact, global competitiveness is maintained by low wages paid to women, hindering any effort to improve wages and working conditions for women in many parts of the world from garment factories in Bangladesh (Berik & van der Meulen Rodgers, 2010) to the maquiladoras in Mexico (Hazarika & Otero , 2004). It is true that many highly educated women have benefited in the form of better opportunities in the formal labor market, which has created greater inequalities among women. But they too have been subject to the glass ceiling at work and the double burden of working in paid employment while taking care of their families.

Invitation to reflect: Take a moment to reflect on the clothes you have in your closet and where they might have been made. Would you be willing to pay a few dollars more and have one fewer T-shirt so that women working in these factories could have a higher wage or better work conditions?

Over the last few decades, women have played a bigger role in the global labor market in agriculture. Reduction in food subsidies and trade liberalization in agriculture has led to increased participation of female labor in agro-export commodities for the same reasons that they are hired in manufacturing export industries as mentioned above. In Latin America, women are taking on more responsibility for subsistence agriculture (Deere, 2009) as men are moving away to the urban areas looking for work. In India and other parts of Asia, women, especially those from historically marginalized groups such as scheduled castes, are increasingly being hired as landless seasonal laborers at very low wages (Breman, 2010).

Women have also entered the service sector in large numbers, but many of the jobs in this sector have been low-paying jobs, especially since the 2008 financial crisis. Global economic integration has led to the commodification of the care economy. As more women have entered the labor market, many activities that have traditionally been done by women in the home have become commodified, such as paid nannies, sex workers, providers of elder care, etc. As a result, there has been an increase in care services in the formal economy, and women are disproportionately represented in these occupations. For example, in the United States only 4% of all workers were employed in paid care services as compared to 20% in 1998 (Folbre & Nelson, 2000). It is hard to gain cost efficiencies in care work without severely compromising on quality, which has led to untenable options such as using low-cost migrant labor or tolerating unregulated, unsafe care conditions.

In response to the greater demand for care services in high income countries and lack of viable employment opportunities in low-income countries, there has been an increase in female migration from mostly low-income countries to high income countries (Beneria et al., 2012). Traditionally when we talk about causal factors in migration, we classify them into push factors and pull factors. The major pull factor is the "care deficit" that exists in Western industrialized countries. As increasing numbers of middle and upper-class women enter the formal labor market, the work that they would typically do in the home (private sphere) such as taking care of children, the sick, and the elderly, and domestic work is left unattended. In addition, the demographic aging of the population in many high-income countries has led to increased need for eldercare. Although things are changing, the research shows that, for the most part, men are not stepping up to take on these chores.

The government has been cutting back on social services because of the neoliberal economic model that is increasingly being adopted across the world. Most of the time, employers are not providing "family friendly" support such as day care facilities or flexible hours. Therefore, a care deficit results in a demand for workers in these occupations. Those tasks that used to happen unremunerated in the private sphere are commodified and become remunerated work in the public sphere. However, most of the time these jobs are still considered women's work and as such have less value placed on them. These jobs often occur either in the home or under illegal circumstances. The work is often invisible, which means that it is less subject to regulation and oversight. As a result, the pay is low, conditions of work are often poor, and there is greater likelihood of exploitation.

Poverty and lack of alternatives push women into these occupations (Ehrenreich & Hochschild, 2003). In addition, women might also be escaping domestic violence, lack of family support, and lack of independence. Governments of the sending countries also encourage emigration of women because they are more likely to send back remittances to their families. These remittances help the children and families of the emigrants, but also help revenue-short governments. I reflect on the irony of my writing this book (while on sabbatical in India) being made possible by the domestic labor of a migrant woman from Nepal. She cooks and cleans, which allows me to write about her oppression. She is here because she supports her family back in Nepal with her income. Ehrenreich & Hochschild (2003) argue that this dependence of the First World on the Third World for care services is a gendered relationship with the undervalued "female" jobs occurring in the Third World, which makes it possible for women and men in the First World to perform the privileged "male" jobs.

World of Unpaid Work

Unpaid work includes a variety of activities that are performed without monetary compensation. These activities are mostly performed in the home in the form of domestic chores like cooking and cleaning, childcare, elder care, and care for the sick. Unpaid work also includes subsistence work on a family farm or family business. It also includes volunteer activities. According to the ILO (2019), across the world, in every single country, women spend more time on unpaid care work than men. On average, women spend four hours and 37 minutes per day on unpaid care work. Globally, women spend about three times as many hours on unpaid domestic work and care work as men. They estimate that the value of this unpaid work is about 11% of global GDP. Pre-pandemic, in many high-income countries, unpaid work by women has declined and paid work has increased. In most high-income countries time-saving domestic technologies in the form of domestic appliances has reduced the amount of time spent on domestic chores. There has also been a shift of care activities from unpaid work in the home to paid work mostly performed by immigrant women as discussed in the earlier section. In some countries in Africa, Asia, and Latin America unpaid work by women has increased. Globally, before the pandemic, the average time per day spent on unpaid work by women decreased by 10 minutes over the last 15 years, while the average time per day spent on unpaid work by men increased by one minute.

Invitation to reflect: Take a moment to reflect on the ways in which your life is dependent on the unpaid or underpaid work of others. How does it make you feel?

When addressing problems of poverty, malnourishment, and morbidity, it has always been assumed that because these strike both men and women there is no need for gender-based analysis. Usually the family or the household is taken as the primary unit of analysis. But the systematic inferior position of women inside and outside the household in many societies points to the necessity of treating gender as a dimension of its own. The poverty of female-headed households is a problem both of female deprivation and family poverty. Males and females in the same family may experience poverty differently, making the position of women in poorer families even more precarious. Evidence shows that despite the biological advantage women have over men in terms of survival and longevity (106 women to 100 men) in many low-income countries there are less women than men (97 to 100). Asia has one of the lowest female male sex ratios so that if the sex ratio corresponded to that of North America or Africa there would be 30 million more women in India and 38 million more women in China today (missing women). In addition, we find that boys benefit more than girls from investments in social services such as health care, education, and childcare (United Nations, 2015). These findings are not just limited to South Asia. A study from sub-Saharan Africa shows that women are more likely to be undernourished than men and that at least half of undernourished women and children are found in nonpoor households (Brown et al., 2017).

Intra-Household Bargaining Model

To better understand these findings, we have to look at the household as a possible site for the creation and perpetuation of gender inequities. In most of the economics literature on the household, it has been assumed that either all members of the household act as one person with the same preferences, goals, and level of utility or there is a household head with everyone's interests in mind (altruistic dictator). More recently, the bargaining models of the household see the household as sites of cooperative conflicts where the interdependencies and social pressures make it fruitful for different parties to cooperate but the division of the fruits that emerge from such cooperation reflects the bargaining power of the respective parties. Sen's (1990) intra-household bargaining model based on the notion of cooperative conflict is one such model. According to this model, prosperity of the household depends on the totality of various activities such as paid employment, purchasing or directly producing food and other goods, providing care to family members, and so on. The members of a household face two different types of problems simultaneously. One of them involves cooperation (adding to total availabilities) and the other involves conflict (dividing the total availabilities among the household members). The sexual division of labor is a part of social arrangements that determine who does what, who gets to consume what, etc. Women tend to have a lower bargaining position because they often have fewer alternatives and have a diminished perception of their own contributions to the household and their own entitlements. As a result, women and girl children often end up with a lower share of household resources and lower decision-making power. According to Sen's model, having access to alternative options through property ownership or wage employment might increase their bargaining position within the household. A better perception of women's work and women's self-worth might also improve women's bargaining position in the household. One way of thinking about it is in terms of what we as women think about the value of our contributions and what they entitle us to, which is conditioned by social norms and the cultural values that perpetuate them. These social norms represent social consensus (coerced or internalized) about the value of specific categories of people and who gets what and why. This consensus develops via socialization and is based on systems of patriarchy and capital accumulation. It also embodies ideas of distributional justice or lack thereof shared by members of a society.

Does Access to Wage Employment Empower Women?

Beneria et al. (2016) and others (Pearson, 2007) question Sen's conclusion that women's participation in wage employment will lead to empowerment via an improved bargaining position within the household. They argue that women's participation in paid work has several effects that operate simultaneously and sometimes in opposite directions. Firstly, it can have a *liberating effect* where women with access to wage employment are empowered in that they are no longer dependent on others for their livelihoods. Feminist researchers have found that access to wage employment can empower women to make life decisions that improve their own lives and that of their children. For example, women working in Columbia's flower industry were able to either negotiate more equitable relations within the household or were able to leave abusive marriages because of their access to wage employment (Friedemann-Sanchez, 2006). Another example from Bangladesh demonstrates that women working in export industries in Bangladesh had great decision-making capability regarding marriage and fertility decisions.

Secondly, inclusion of women into wage employment can intensify unequal gender relations. For example, in Taiwan and Japan, women workers continued to play the role of obedient daughters by sending most of their incomes back home to their families (Takenoshita, 2012). The nature of the employment needs to be considered as well. Employment that is exploitative and conducted under inhumane working conditions can substantially reduce women's agency. In India, as part of our study of women working in the informal labor market in Mumbai (Basu & Thomas, 2009), we found that women construction workers dealt with sexual harassment and sexual assault daily. They were unable to stand up to it because they had no other options. They needed employment to make ends meet but now were subject to gender violence at home and in the workplace. In addition, in most cases, when women enter paid work, they continue to be responsible for taking care of their families. For example, in commuter trains in Mumbai, women returning home from work have been observed chopping vegetables they bought on the way from their place of work to the train station in preparation for dinner that night. By contrast, men are often observed playing cards on the ride home as a form of release from their stressful day!

The solution is not to take away those employment opportunities but to ensure that workers, both men and women, work in safe, healthy environments and get paid a wage commensurate to their work. Women have sometimes been able to get paid to do work that allows them to express their creativity and make a living. In a shout-out to grandmothers, here are two stories from Cambodia and India about grandmothers who have shown us the way. Silk weaving in Cambodia is an ancient art that has been passed down from mother to daughter for centuries. The French and Japanese occupation, the brutality of the Pol Pot regime, and then the Vietnamese occupation disrupted all normal life in Cambodia for over 100 years. In 1996, seven silk grandmothers, as they were called, started working in a silk studio set up on the tourist route to Angkor Wat.

They revived this ancient art form, brought their daughters and granddaughters to work with them while they taught them this skill, and created beautiful textiles that honored their values and ancestral wisdom while also being economically profitable.

Another story from India is about Barefoot College, started by Sanjit Roy, which combines local traditional knowledge and skills with more modern technologies to educate people to become teachers and engineers and architects. The entire college is solar-powered with the system being designed and constructed by a local villager with eight years of formal education. The college then trained and educated other villagers, primarily grandmothers to install solar power in the entire village. They invested and trained grandmothers to be their solar power engineers because the grandmothers are mature, wise, and most likely to give back to their communities. They have now installed solar power in over 600 villages in India. They have also trained grandmothers in other countries in Asia and Africa. When a local woman was asked about how she had benefited from solar power, she said that for the first time she could see her husband's face in the winter (Singer & Ricard, 2015).

British feminist economist Ruth Pearson (2007) also discusses women's access to microcredit as a strategy for women's empowerment. Microcredit has created opportunities for women to be entrepreneurial and improve their lives. They seem to be especially successful when the loans have been taken by groups of women working as cooperatives, spreading the risk of nonrepayment over multiple borrowers. Many of the microcredit organizations also offer literacy programs and health programs initiated by women who have recognized that to be successful, women's work in the public and private domains need to be recognized. But there are also times when having access to microcredit have not led to women's empowerment. In some cases, men end up controlling the funds while women end up with the debts. In a lot of cases, other factors such as the incidence of HIV or death of family members means that the women are not able to repay the loans and are therefore shut out of these opportunities.

Global Financial Crisis of 2008

Overall, the global financial crisis led to a significant decline in global GDP (-2.5%) and world trade (-9.86%). Indian economist Jayati Ghosh (2011) argues that financial crises disproportionately affect those that benefited the least from the boom. In other words, the most vulnerable segments of the economy are the ones who are most likely to suffer from unemployment and loss of provision of public services. With the most recent financial crisis, there was a decline in export-oriented production, most of which is done by female labor. Thousands of women around the world lost their jobs from Cambodia (Dasgupta & Williams, 2010) to Argentina to Mexico (Esquivel & Rodriguez Enriquez, 2014). In addition, there was a decline in services in the care economy and other forms of informal work, which is another area dominated by women. The recent financial crisis was also followed by a loss in public services as tax revenues dwindled. A loss in public services often means that those services will need to be done in the household instead, which increases the burden on women and children who do most of the household production. Finally, material deprivation for men often leads to greater frustration, which results in increased violence against women.

Economic Impact of COVID-19

Using the basic Susceptible, Infectious, and/or Recovered (SIR) model (Kermack & McKendrick, 1927), economists have identified the theoretical aggregate supply and aggregate demand effects that pandemics have on the economy. Aggregate supply decreases as production shuts down due to risk of infection from working in high contact jobs. Aggregate demand decreases because consumption shuts down due to risk of infection from consuming high contact goods and services. Secondary decreases in demand occur due to loss of income and uncertainty. Secondary decreases in supply occur due to loss of profit and uncertainty. Unemployment and loss of income leads to housing distress and loan defaults, which in turn could affect the financial and banking sector. The outcome is not efficient because of consumption and production externalities, i.e., people do not take into account the impact of their own actions on the infection rates of others. Therefore, policy recommendations include lockdown measures to contain the spread of the infection. This exacerbates the recession but saves lives (studies have shown that 250,000 to 500,000 lives were saved in the US). Second phase policy recommendation is to open the economy with monitored safety protocol, such as mandatory face covering and social distancing, which saves lives and helps economic recovery. Unemployment benefits and other direct income transfers flatten the economic recession. Liquidity assistance to firms and payment deferment alleviate housing distress in the short term.

According to World Bank Data this model played out in our lives with the pandemic leading to a devastating decline in global GDP (-4.28%), world trade (-8.9%), and oil prices in 2020. Global capital outflows from emerging market economies (EMEs) in the first half of 2020 led to a depreciation in the exchange rates for the currencies of EMEs and an appreciation in the exchange rates for currencies of high-income economies. Global merchandise trade recorded its sharpest ever one-period decline in the second quarter, falling 14.3%. The steepest declines were in Europe and North America, where exports fell 24.5% and 21.8%, respectively. By comparison, Asian exports were relatively unaffected, dropping just 6.1%. During the same period imports were down 14.5% in North America and 19.3% in Europe but just 7.1% in Asia. The decline in the services trade during the pandemic has been at least as strong as the fall in merchandise trade. There has been a much steeper decline in global trade in services during the current recession (-23%) than during the financial crisis (-9%). The plunge was exacerbated by restrictions on international travel, which represents a key source of export earnings for many low-income countries. Although the trade decline during the COVID-19 pandemic is similar in magnitude to the global financial crisis of 2008–2009, the economic context is very different. The contraction in GDP has been much stronger in the current recession, while the fall in trade has been more moderate. Lockdowns and travel restrictions drastically reduced output and employment in non-traded services. At the same time, robust monetary and fiscal policies have propped up incomes, allowing consumption and imports to rebound once lockdowns were eased.

According to the World Trade Organization data the impact of the pandemic was uneven across industries. Automotive products recorded the biggest decline of any category (-70% in April 2020). Travel goods, clothing, footwear also recorded a steep decline in April since this category includes a large proportion of luxury goods. Computers and information technology infrastructure and pharmaceuticals rose during the pandemic. Not surprisingly, trade in personal protective equipment (PPE) recorded explosive growth, up 92% in the second quarter and 122% in May. The pandemic has also exacerbated existing inequalities. By September 2020, high-income countries had spent $695 per capita on social protection whereas low-income countries had spent $4 per capita. According to UN Women data from 45 countries, women were less likely to receive cash relief (17%) as compared to men (27%). The total earnings of workers fell in 2020 by $3.7 trillion, whereas the wealth of global billionaires increased by $3.9 trillion. It reflects the depth of our moral and spiritual bankruptcy that a global crisis of this proportion that has taken millions of lives and billions of livelihoods has left some richer beyond their dreams. A crisis can evoke our compassion and bring us together or it can evoke fear and greed and tear us apart. We have allowed yet another crisis to tear us apart.

Loss of Jobs

According to estimates from the ILO, more than a 100 million jobs were lost globally during 2020. Adding in the potential job growth we would have experienced in the absence of a pandemic as well as the reduction in work hours for those who continued to be employed, the total loss in terms of working hours was equivalent to 255 million full time jobs for a year. The resulting decline in incomes along with very limited social safety nets increased global poverty levels, wherein an additional 108 million workers are now in poverty, living on less than $3.50 per day in purchasing power terms, as compared to 2019. Women were much harder hit (4.2%) compared to men (3.0%) unlike the 2008 economic crisis. Across all country income levels, the employment to population ratio for women fell by 3.8% in 2020 whereas the employment to population ratio for men fell by 3.3%, increasing the gender gap in employment to population ratios across the world. Women tend to be disproportionately represented in those sectors that were hardest hit by the pandemic (retail, hospitality, domestic work, garment manufacturing). For example, 80% of workers in the garment industry are women, and almost 73 million jobs in the garment and textile industries were at risk during the pandemic. I reflect on our interdependence when I remember that during 2020 and much of 2021 I spent much less on clothes and shoes because working from home meant that I did not need them as much. It is significant to note that our cumulative reduction in demand led to millions of jobs being lost around the world, especially those done by women.

Young workers (aged 15 to 24 years) were much harder hit by the pandemic than adult workers. According to ILO estimates from a sample of 35 high-income countries, the drop in employment of young women (11.8%) was almost double that of young men (5.8%), and far more than that of adult women (0.8%) and adult men (0.6%). Young women tend to have lower labor force attachment and tend to be in the informal economy, which means that it was easier to let them go. Workers in the informal economy account for two out of three workers globally, including 740 million women who were three times as likely to lose their jobs as compared to those in the formal economy. It also means that they had no access to social safety nets. The pandemic also had a disproportionate impact on low-skilled workers as compared to high-skilled workers. Higher skilled workers were able to adapt to working virtually more easily and, along with access to digital connectivity, were not as likely to lose their jobs as compared to lower skill workers who were either laid off or were on the front lines with greater exposure to the virus. Domestic workers, especially migrant workers who are mostly women, were disproportionately affected by the pandemic in terms of job loss and reduced work hours.

Invitation to reflect: Take a moment to reflect on the ways in which your life was affected by the changes discussed above.

Even worse, the modest recovery that we have observed since 2020 has not benefited women where the growth in real GDP is negatively correlated with women's employment growth. ILO (2021) predictions suggest that while men's employment will recover to pre-pandemic levels, women's employment will not recover to the tune of 13 million fewer jobs in 2021 compared to 2019. This pattern is not unlike what we have observed with other crises. Almost 90% of women who lost their jobs ended up quitting the labor force, which along with their unpaid care responsibilities makes it much harder for them to reenter the labor force. Women's labor force participation is projected to remain below pre-pandemic levels in 169 countries around the world in 2022. According to UN Women (2022), "By the end of 2022, around 383 million women and girls will live in extreme poverty compared to 368 million men and boys. If current trends continue, by 2030, more women and girls will live in extreme poverty in sub-Saharan Africa than do today."

Loss of jobs and supply chain disruptions has also led to rising food insecurity. Before the pandemic, women were already 27% more likely to be food insecure than men. The pandemic is predicted to have increased that gap even further. School closures and lockdowns have also meant that women have taken on the bulk of the increased care giving responsibilities. Not surprisingly there is a substantial increase in the number of hours of unpaid work for women worldwide. The crucial role that care services play in the economy and in our lives was sharply revealed during this pandemic in ways that we have never experienced before. In the next chapter we will focus on the care economy and the absolute imperative that we recognize and acknowledge its importance and be willing to fund it in a sustainable way.

Key Takeaways

Below are the key ideas to take away from this chapter:

- During the last 50 years, we have experienced an unprecedented intensification of global economic integration in the form of expanded flows of trade, capital, finance, and people across borders.
- One of the major consequences of expansion of markets has been growing inequalities wherein some have prospered but the majority have experienced greater insecurity and environmental degradation.
- As markets have expanded, more and more women have engaged in paid employment accompanied by increased informalization of the labor market and commodification of the care economy.
- Women's participation in paid work has empowered them in some cases but has intensified unequal gender relations in other cases.
- The financial crisis of 2008 disproportionately affected those that benefited the least from the boom.
- The pandemic has not only claimed millions of lives, but it has also exacerbated existing inequalities in income and exposed the precarity of the care economy and social protections.

Comprehension Questions

Directions: Use what you have learned in this chapter to help you respond to the questions below:

1. In what ways has global economic integration exacerbated economic inequalities?

2. Beneria, Sen, and Pearson give us different perspectives on the impact of women's inclusion into the market economy on women's empowerment. Use these perspectives to compare and contrast the extent to which women's inclusion in income generating activities has improved their lives.
3. Why do Ehrenreich & Hochschild argue that the dependence of the First World on the Third World for care services is a gendered relationship?
4. Why did Ghosh argue that the financial crisis of 2008 disproportionately affected those that benefited the least from the boom?
5. In what ways did women bear the brunt of this pandemic?

References

Alliance for Affordable Internet (2021). The costs of exclusion: Economic consequences of the digital gender gap. Web Foundation.

Basu, R. & Thomas, M. (2009). Exploring women's daily lives and participation in the informal labor market in Mumbai. *Gender and Development, 17*(2), 231–242.

Benería, L., Berik, G., & Floro, M. (2016). *Gender, Development, and Globalization: Economics as if All People Mattered* (2nd ed.). Routledge.

Beneria, L., Deere, C, & Kabeer, N. (2012). Gender and international migration: Globalization, development and governance. *Feminist Economics,* 18(2), 1–34.

Berik, G. & van der Meulen Rodgers, Y. (2010). Options for Enforcing Labour Standards: Lessons from Bangladesh and Cambodia. *Journal of International Development,* 22(1), 56–85.

Breman, J. (2010). *Outcast Labor in Asia—Circulation and Informalization of the Workforce at the Bottom of the Economy.* Oxford University Press.

Brown, C., Ravallion, M., & van de Walle D. (2017). Are poor individuals mainly found in poor households? Evidence using nutrition data for Africa. NBER Working Paper No. 24047, National Bureau of Economic Research.

Dasgupta, S. & Williams, D. (2010). Women facing the economic crisis—The garment sector in Cambodia. In A. Bauer & M. Thant (Eds.), *Poverty and Sustainable Development in Asia.* Manila: Asian Development Bank.

Deere, C. (2009). The feminization of agriculture? The impact of economic restructuring in rural Latin America. In Shahra Razavi (Ed*), The Gendered Impacts of Liberalization: Towards Embedded Liberalism?* (pp. 99–127). Routledge.

Diffenbaugh, N. & Burke, M. (2019). Global warming has increased global economic inequality. *Proceedings of the National Academy of Sciences of the United States of America,* 116(20), 9808–9813.

Ehrenreich, B. & Hochschild, A. (2003). *Global Woman: Nannies, Maids, and Sex Workers in the New Economy.* New York: Metropolitan Books.

Esquivel, V. & Rodriguez Enriquez, C. (2014). Addressing the global economic crisis in Mexico, Ecuador and Argentina: Implications for gender equality. In Rania Antonopoulos (Ed.), *Gender Perspectives and the Gender Impacts of the Global Economic Crisis.* Routledge.

Friedemann-Sanchez, G. (2006). Assets in intrahousehold bargaining among women in Colombia's cut flower industry. Feminist Economics, 12(1-2), 247–69.

Folbre, N. & Nelson, J. (2000). For love or money—or both? *Journal of Economic Perspectives,* 14(4), 123–140.

Ghosh, J. (2011). Financial crises and the impact on women: A historical note. In N. Visvanathan, L. Duggan, N. Wiegersma, & L. Nisonoff (Eds). *The Women, Gender and Development Reader* (2nd ed.). Zed Books.

Hazarika, G., & Otero, R. (2004). Foreign trade and the gender earnings differential in urban Mexico. *Journal of Economic Integration,* 19(2), 353–73.

International Labour Office (2019). *The unpaid care work and the labour market. An analysis of time use data based on the latest World Compilation of Time-use Surveys.* Geneva: ILO.

ILO Policy Brief (2021). An uneven and gender-unequal COVID-19 recovery: Update on gender and employment trends 2021.

Kermack, W. & McKendrick A. (1927). A contribution to the mathematical theory of epidemics. *Proceedings of the Royal Society,* 115, 700–72.

Lakner, C., & Milanović, B. (2016). Global income distribution. From the fall of the Berlin Wall to the Great Recession. *World Bank Economic Review,* World Bank Group, 30(2), 203–232.

Lopez, R. & Miller, S. (2008). Chile: The unbearable burden of inequality. *World Development,* 36(12), 2679–95.

Maquilapolis: City of Factories. (2006). Princeton, NJ.: Films for the Humanities & Sciences.

McMichael, P. (2012). The land grab and corporate food regime restructuring. *Journal of Peasant Studies,* 39(3–4), 681–701.

Mohanty, C. (2003). *Feminism Without Borders: Decolonizing Theory, Practicing Solidarity.* Duke University Press.

Pearson, R. (2007). Reassessing paid work and women's empowerment: Lessons from the global economy. In A. Cornwall, E. Harrison, & A. Whitehead (Eds.). *Feminisms in Development: Contradictions, Contestations and Challenges.* Zed Books.

Peet, R. (2011). Inequality, crisis and austerity in finance capitalism. *Cambridge Journal of Regions, Economy and Society,* 4(3), 383–99.

Sen, A. (1990). Gender and cooperative conflicts. In Irene Tinker (Ed.) *Persistent Inequalities.* Oxford University Press.

Shorrocks, A., Davies, J. & Lluberas, R. (2018). *Global Wealth Report 2018.* Credit Suisse Research Institute, Credit Suisse.

Singer, T. & Ricard, M. (2015). *Caring Economics: Conversations on Altruism and Compassion, Between Scientists, Economists, and the Dalai Lama.* Picador.

Takenoshita, H. (2012). Family, labour market structures and the dynamics of self-employment in three Asian countries: Gender differences in self-employment entry in Japan, Korea and Taiwan. *Comparative Social Research,* 29, 85–112.
United Nations. (2015). The World's Women 2015: Trends and Statistics.
UN Women (2022). Progress on the Sustainable Development Goals: The Gender Snapshot 2022. UN Women and Women Count.
World Social Report (2020). *Inequality in the Rapidly Changing World.* Department of Economic and Social Affairs, United Nations.

Chapter 7

Reframing the Care Economy

Toward a More Just and Compassionate World

> The openness of our hearts and minds can be measured by how wide we draw the circle of what we call family.
>
> —Mother Teresa, Albanian–Indian Catholic nun, recipient of the Nobel Peace Prize, 1979

From Local Stories to Global Visions

The Russian invasion of Ukraine in 2022 has forced many Ukrainians, mostly women and children, to flee to Poland. The Polish government has taken them in, but it has further exacerbated the care crisis in Poland. One such story was reported in the New York Times in April 2022. Ukrainian refugee Lubomira Pancuk, a mother of three, expressed her gratitude for the support she has received from the Polish government and her Polish neighbors, but stated that she is unable to find care services for her three-week-old son. Without those care services she cannot take up a job and support her family. Care services for children under the age of three were expensive and hard to find in Poland even before the Ukrainian refugee crisis. While many day care providers want to help Ukrainian refugees and their children, they don't have the capacity to meet this need without creating more shortages for Polish families. More refugees are showing up every day, exposing the fragile nature of the care economy in Poland.

Invitation to reflect: Take a moment to reflect on the dilemma that Lubomira faces with respect to finding care services for her son while being displaced by the war.

Introduction

In chapter 6, we discussed the ways in which systems of oppression continue to manifest themselves in the economic lives of women, men, and children in the labor market and in the household today. We discussed the ways in which the global financial crisis of 2008 and the global public health crisis (COVID-19 pandemic) have exacerbated economic inequalities between men and women in the labor market and in the household. We discussed that the care crisis, jobs crisis, and climate crisis are all interconnected and have a significantly greater impact on women. In the next three chapters, we start the work of visioning and reimagining another path forward that will take us toward a more just and compassionate world. We will look back at the lessons we have learned from earlier chapters and use them as the foundation for a new vision. In this chapter, we will focus on the care crisis that the pandemic has accelerated and discuss ways in which the care economy can be valued and funded to create the conditions for a just and compassionate recovery.

As discussed earlier, let us put the myth of individualism to rest once and for all. We are all dependent on each other and require care from each other to survive. None of us could have survived to adulthood if someone hadn't taken care of us, fed us, and sheltered us. And as adults there will be times in our lives when we will be sick, when we might be incapacitated, when we will most likely age to the point of needing more intensive care. During those times in our lives, we are at our most vulnerable and need care and compassion from each other.

Invitation to reflect: Take a moment to reflect on a time in your life when you needed and received care from someone else. Who was this person? How did it feel to receive care from another human being?

Most of the time that care is provided by women within a paid or unpaid context. Not only have we not assumed care as a collective responsibility of all human beings, but we have continued to underpay, undervalue, and exploit the labor that women put into care work. If this pandemic has taught us one lesson, it must be that care work can no longer be considered private and feminized. In this chapter, we will discuss a new feminist and compassionate plan for assuming care work as a shared responsibility. Given the externalities and high cost of providing high-quality care, it must be treated as a public good and therefore be funded by the state. Investing in publicly funded universal care services will not only provide the infrastructure necessary for all human life to flourish, but it will also generate stable well-paid jobs and help achieve gender equality. It will also help decrease inequalities in health, education, and income and make us more resilient and prepared for future crises.

Key Takeaways from Earlier Chapters

Let's take a moment to pause and look back at the lessons we have learned from earlier chapters—lessons to lay the foundations for a vision of a more just and compassionate world. From chapter 1, we learned that social justice requires that all people have the same rights and are treated fairly so that it leads to equitable opportunities and equitable outcomes for all. The unprecedented upheaval in our economic and social structures over the last three years has had a devastating effect on gender equality, but it has also provided us with an opportunity to envision a different path forward that addresses the triple crises of job loss, climate change, and a fractured care economy. Compassion and social justice are intimately tied together, and each is necessary for the other to exist. We need to save the world not because we are angry or guilty or fearful, but because we love it and we belong to it and each other.

From chapters 2 and 3, we learned that economic growth does not always lead to greater well-being. Feminist economists see development as a process that provides for the survival, sustenance, and flourishing of life. Feminist economists explicitly acknowledge, recognize, and demonstrate the interdependent and interconnected nature of care work. The COVID-19 pandemic has highlighted the inequitable way in which the economy relies on the unpaid labor of mostly women in the care economy. The feminist definition of development places the care economy in the center of the analysis. Accordingly, economic success in terms of outcomes should be measured not by real GDP per capita, but by the well-being of all people, especially the most marginalized in society. Well-being is a much broader concept than economic growth and brings attention to the composition and distribution of resources. It also identifies productive work as that which creates the conditions for all people to survive, thrive, and flourish. Economic success is measured not only in terms of outcomes but also in terms of more equitable participation by all people in all aspects of economic, political, and social life. Acknowledging intersectionality regarding race, class, sexual orientation, and other social identities challenges notions about the homogeneity of women's experiences and allows for a richer and more inclusive understanding of women's experiences across space and time. Feminists define economic development as a process of *social provisioning,* which calls for greater focus on the synergies between sustainability and gender justice and putting care for all people and care for the planet front and center.

From chapter 4 we learned that we need to make gender the central category of analysis and social provisioning the chief activity under study. We need to make visible the ways in which the unpaid/underpaid work of mostly women contribute to social provisioning and social reproduction. From chapter 5 we learned that men exploit women to appropriate the surplus generated by women. Women are also exploited by capital in their role as housewives and in their role as wage labor. We also learned that violence is used to initiate and perpetuate systems of oppression. As feminists, we intentionally and thoughtfully choose not to use violence and tools of oppression to advance our vision. Instead, we seek to create a world with no hierarchies, where no one is exploited or oppressed. We choose compassion and the wisdom of our lived experiences to dismantle oppressive systems. The compassionate approach demands that everyone is included and everyone belongs. It also demands that we do this work out of love, not hate.

From chapter 6 we learned that the pandemic has not only claimed millions of lives, but it has also exacerbated existing inequalities in income and exposed the precarity of the care economy and social protections. Women were harder hit in terms of job loss, lack of social protections, and increased hours of unpaid work. Almost 90% of women who lost their jobs ended up quitting the labor force, which along with their unpaid care responsibilities makes it much harder for them to re-enter the labor force. Loss of jobs and supply chain disruptions has also led to rising food insecurity. Before the pandemic, women were already 27% more likely to be food insecure than men. The pandemic is predicted to have increased that gap even further. School closures and lockdowns have also meant that women have taken on the bulk of the increased caregiving responsibilities. Not surprisingly, there is a substantial increase in the number of hours of unpaid work for women worldwide. The crucial role that care services play in the economy and in our lives was sharply revealed during this pandemic in unprecedented ways.

What Is the Care Economy?

Care work is required at those times in our lives when we have limited ability to take care of ourselves and have to depend on other human beings for care. As children we need to be fed, cleaned, hugged, swaddled, and clothed because we are unable to do these tasks for ourselves. When we are sick or elderly, we might need help brushing our hair, being turned from one side to another as we lay in a bed, being hand fed our food, being helped out of a bed into a wheelchair, having our toenails cut and our skin moisturized, and doing myriad other tasks that we often take for granted when we are reasonably healthy and active adults. All these activities are considered part of care work. It is important to recognize that those who receive care are not entirely helpless. They are often able to enrich the lives of their caregivers and others in qualitatively different ways. For example, studies have shown that both men and women who have close, meaningful care interactions with their children live longer and have better health outcomes than those who do not (MenCare, 2017). Caring for my child gave me the opportunity to deeply connect with another human being and taught me many life lessons that I would not have learned without her. She continues to make me a better person every day, which is gratifying, but it is also important for this work to be recognized and compensated.

Invitation to reflect: Take a moment to reflect on a time in your life when *you* provided care to someone else. Who was this person? How did it feel to provide care to another human being?

According to Iranian born economist Shahra Razavi (2007), "**Care work involves direct care of persons; it can be paid or unpaid. Those with intense care needs include young children, the frail, the elderly, and people with other illnesses and disabilities.**" Other household activities such as shopping, cooking, cleaning, and washing are not considered to be care work. Instead, they are considered to be pre-conditions to care work, although this distinction can sometimes be arbitrary and blurred. Care work happens in different contexts. It can be in the form of (a) unpaid care provided by families and households, (b) paid care provided by the market, (c) paid care provided by the state, and (d) care (both paid and unpaid) provided by the not-for-profit/community sector. This has been called the diamond of caregiving responsibilities or the care diamond.

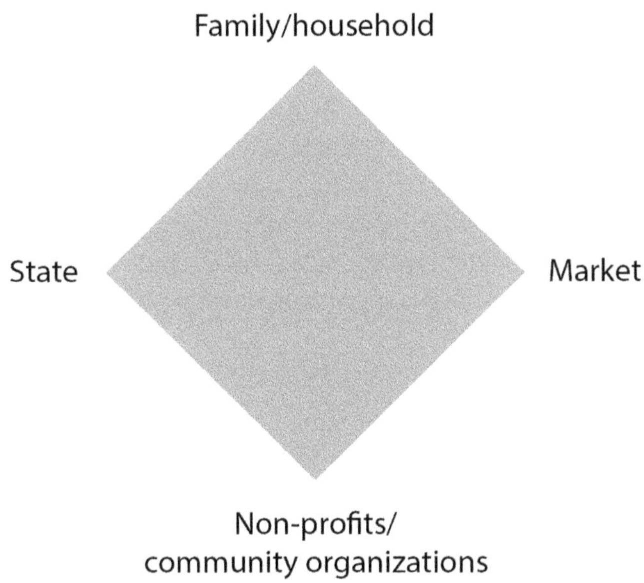

Figure 7.1 The Diamond of Caregiving Responsibilities (Adapted from Shahra Razavi, "The Political and Social Economy of Care in a Development Context: Conceptual Issues, Research Questions and Policy Options," *Gender and Development Programme Paper Number 3.* Copyright © 2007 by United Nations Research Institute for Social Development.

Relationship Between Paid Care and Unpaid Care

One way to think about the relationship between paid care and unpaid care is in terms of how we spend our time. We have to feed ourselves, clean ourselves, and care for ourselves and others (mostly unpaid). We also work in the market economy (paid economy) to generate an income, which enables us to buy goods and services that we need. The more time we spend on any one of these activities the less time we have for other activities. If we spend more time in the market economy, then some activities, including care activities, will either have to move into the paid economy or be done in less time with productivity enhancements. For example, we have to wash our clothes so we could do it ourselves (unpaid) or give it to a laundry service (paid economy) or hire someone to come into the home to do it (paid economy) or buy a washing machine to reduce the amount of time and effort spent on the task. Historically these productivity enhancements have been more possible in unpaid housework than in unpaid care work. As a result, care work accounts for an increasing share of unpaid work, especially in high income countries (Himmelweit, 2005).

Globally 16.4 billion hours are spent on unpaid care work every day, which is the equivalent of 2 billion people working without pay for eight hours per day. If they were remunerated at the global minimum wage it would account for 9% of global GDP. Most unpaid care work continues to happen in the home and is primarily done by women. It imposes costs such as foregone wage and employment opportunities. According to the ILO (2018), while there are significant differences between countries, globally women perform 76.2% of all unpaid care work. In the United States, women perform 61.1% of unpaid care work. While men's contribution to unpaid care work has increased in some countries the gender gap in unpaid care work has declined by only seven minutes between 1997 and 2012 (ILO 2018). At this rate it will take more than 200 years to close the gender gap in unpaid care work. The pandemic has further increased the unequal pressure on women, who are now spending an additional 5.2 hours per week on childcare alone. To be able to provide care in the home at the specific times of the day that it is needed requires job flexibility, part time hours, jobs with lower promotion possibilities which happen to be in sectors that pay far less than other jobs. This is one of the explanations for the gender wage gap. Unequal participation in unpaid care work results in unequal outcomes in the labor market. According to the ILO (2018) the "motherhood employment penalty" borne by mothers with children below the age of five results in this group having the lowest employment rate (47.6%) compared to fathers of young children who have the highest employment rate (87.9%). If we do not address inequalities in unpaid care work, we will not be able to achieve gender equality in other areas.

Invitation to reflect: Take a moment to reflect on the impact of unpaid care responsibilities on your salary and possibilities for promotion. If you don't have a job, consider this question in terms of one of your female family members.

According to the ILO (2018) when countries spend more on care services, maternal labor force participation rates increase, allowing women to participate in the paid economy more fully. Public expenditure on care services also leads to greater gender equality in education, health, and labor force outcomes. Despite the evidence, government expenditures on care services remain low in much of Africa, Asia, and the Middle East.

Over the last 50 years as women are increasingly spending more time in the market economy, care work has shifted from unpaid work to paid work, with mostly women doing this work as day care workers, nurses, elder care providers, domestic workers, nannies, and so on. For example, professional care services in the United States employed 4% of all workers in 1900 as compared to 20% in 1998 (Folbre & Nelson, 2000). Women in low-income households often provide paid care services for higher income households and provide unpaid care services and unpaid housework services for their own households. Lack of running water or electricity in low-income households increase the amount of time spent on unpaid housework. For example, in Latin America and the Caribbean, 12% of rural households do not have electricity and 16% don't have access to drinking water. In many cases, female children take on some of these unpaid responsibilities, leading to lower school attendance and further reducing their life opportunities.

Paid care providers in the market run the gamut from unregulated low-cost, low-wage care facilities that hire predominantly women from marginalized groups and immigrant women in the informal labor market to higher end care facilities in the formal economy. Many middle and higher income households also hire in-home care providers that range from low-skill, low-wage care workers to high skill, higher wage workers. In the low-skill, low-wage end of the spectrum, women are expected to work long hours with no formal contracts or benefits. They don't get paid leave or health benefits, and they enjoy very little job security. There is also very little possibility of training or promotion. Their skills are often undervalued and underpaid. For example, the U.S. Bureau of Labor Statistics reports that in May 2020, the median annual wage ($29,960) of health care support occupations (such as home health aides, occupational therapy assistants, and medical transcriptionists) was lower than the median annual wage for all occupations in the economy. In much of Latin America, the income of domestic workers is less than 50% of the average income of all other occupations.

The paid and unpaid care economy is also plagued with the cost disease (Himmelweit, 2005). There is

no way to improve productivity in this kind of work without reducing the quality of the care. Care work is extremely labor intensive and any attempts to reduce the number of hours spent on care work only results in negligent care, not productivity enhancements. Wage increases elsewhere in the economy put pressure on the wages of care workers, which in turn pushes up the cost of offering these services. The shift of care services from unpaid to paid work in many high-income countries has highlighted the cost disease even more, leading to the dilemma of providing high-quality, high-wage care that would compensate those workers more fairly for their services while increasing the cost of care services with the result of it being more difficult for families to afford these kinds of services. Paid care provided by the state is also subject to the cost disease in many high-income countries (Folbre, 2006). Austerity measures and reductions in government spending over the last several years have led to a reduction in social services. As a result, much of this work has shifted to the unpaid sector within the household and community organizations in many countries. Paid and unpaid care provided by non-governmental organizations of various kinds—from women's collectives to churches and mosques—are often reliant on volunteers at the informal end of the spectrum or paid employees at the high end of the spectrum.

Reframing the Care Economy as the Cornerstone of a Just and Compassionate World

The call to recognize, redistribute, reward, regulate, represent, and reorganize care work is a longstanding feminist demand, framed within the economics discipline by British economist Diane Elson (2017) and others. Some analysts use an instrumental approach to the care economy by reinforcing its importance for economic growth as an investment in human and social capital. Others have looked at it in a much broader way as a basic human right. Care work is one of the most direct ways in which we contribute to the survival, sustenance, and flourishing of life. No other activity is possible without it. In that sense it can be seen as the necessary infrastructure that undergirds the rest of the economy. The well-being literature provides ample evidence that social interaction and prosocial behaviors are some of the most important factors contributing to our well-being (Helliwell et al., 2018). Care work can be one of the most powerful ways in which we can strengthen our social bonds with each other. Receiving and providing care when we need it the most is the essence of building a more compassionate world. When we are cared for and are able to care for others, it not only enhances our well-being (Weng et al., 2013), but it also increases our ability to function more effectively (Gilbert, 2015).

Invitation to reflect: Take a moment to reflect on a time in your life when receiving or providing care strengthened your emotional bond with another human being. How would you describe the value of this experience for you?

As mentioned earlier, while compassion is a natural response, it is also a difficult one that requires intentionality, awareness, and courage. There are many forces that teach and encourage us to compete for scarce resources, to practice othering, and to practice harming each other intentionally or unintentionally in order to survive. In the words of South African President Nelson Mandela, *"If they can learn to hate, they can be taught to love." R*esearch has shown us that compassionate care can be cultivated with training and practice (Leiberg et al., 2011; Kemeny et al., 2012).

Invitation to reflect: Take a moment to reflect on the last time you encountered a homeless individual. Did you feel moved to help in some way? If not, what keeps you from being compassionate and caring toward other human beings?

American economists Nancy Folbre and Julie Nelson (2000) ask about the nature of care provided in intimate relationships that are motivated by money and not love. It is argued that insisting that the care economy needs to be motivated by love has led to exploitation of women where they are the ones expected to be self-sacrificing and altruistic while society does not have the same expectation of men. Folbre and Nelson (2000) argue that compensating workers for their labor does not mean that the work has become purely transactional. It is possible to have rich, meaningful relationships of care within the paid economy. Providing care enhances human capabilities and leads to survival and thriving of life. Providing high-quality care to children at early stages in their development contributes to their thriving and to the greater good of society. Maintaining the dignity and care of the elderly and the disabled is critically important for building trust and creating a community that cares for each other and contributes to greater well-being. The findings of the 2021 World Happiness Report highlight the importance of building trust in each other and in public institutions, especially during crises (Helliwell et al., 2021). They found that countries with higher levels of trust not only had higher levels of well-being but were also more likely to have fewer deaths due to COVID-19.

Invitation to reflect: Take a moment to imagine living in a world where we trusted each other and our public institutions to take care of us when we are at our most vulnerable. How does it make you feel?

Inequalities in the Care Economy

Reframing the care economy places it as a cornerstone of social justice. The distribution and access to high-quality care services is highly unequal and leads to unequal outcomes in all other areas that depend on it. Some of us receive high-quality care as children, which contributes greatly to our life opportunities. Most of us do not receive high-quality care, and as a result, our life chances are significantly reduced, leading to greater inequalities in health outcomes, education outcomes, and career outcomes. This in turn affects the kind of care we have access to later in our lives. It also affects our ability to provide high-quality care to our children, and the cycle continues. In many countries, women from marginalized racial/ethnic groups tend to provide most of the care services demanded by the socially dominant groups, while their own needs for care are disregarded or ignored. In many cases, the care deficit in high income countries is being met by migrant women from low-income countries, leading to the global supply chain in care services. The care deficit in high income countries is a result of inadequate provision of social services by the state, unwillingness by men to take on additional care responsibilities, and more women entering the labor market without employers providing enough support for care activities. The system is providing care to some children but not others; supporting the reproduction and fertility of some groups and not others. In other words, inequalities in the care economy create and perpetuate inequalities in all other areas, making this a fundamental social justice issue that must be addressed if we want to create a more just and compassionate world. Thus, the questions that lay before us are these: How can we provide high quality care to all groups in an equitable way? How can those who provide care be well compensated and valued without the expectation that care work will be done mostly by women? Much of the feminist literature argues that the public provision of universal care services is the best option while acknowledging that it isn't a panacea.

Market Failures in the Care Economy

The failure of the market to provide high-quality care services to all is another argument for public provision of care services. We know that the market for care services is often subject to problems of asymmetrical information, leading to the need for monitoring to ensure quality of care. This leads to high transaction costs and resulting market failures. At the extreme end of the quality-of-care continuum, we find child abuse and elder abuse both in the home and in institutional settings. According to a 2017 study of elder abuse in 28 countries, 15.7% of people over the age of 60 have experienced some form of elder abuse (Yon et al., 2017). Another study about elder abuse in institutional settings found that 64% of staff working in these settings has admitted to perpetrating some form of elder abuse (Yon et al., 2018). Recent evidence suggests that elder abuse increased during the pandemic, in some cases as high as 84% in the United States (Chang & Levy, 2021). Elder abuse has serious consequences for the elderly, including premature mortality and financial devastation, which will only get worse as the population over the age of 60 increases worldwide from 900 million in 2015 to 2 billion in 2050. Poor quality elder care and childcare has consequences for all of us directly as we might well be part of this group, but also indirectly as the strength and health of our communities deteriorate. The presence of these externalities also increases the possibility of market failures. The prevalence of these market failures provides another justification for public provision of care. The public benefits of providing high-quality care far exceed the private benefit to individuals.

Invitation to reflect: Take a moment to reflect on the kind of care that you/your loved ones would like to receive when you/they are above the age of 60.

Crisis in the Care Economy

According to the ILO (2018) there is a looming crisis in the care economy that, if left unaddressed, will lead to an unsustainable global care crisis in the next two decades. The crisis is fueled on the one hand by a shortage of well-trained care workers and on the other hand by an increase in the demand for care services. The ILO estimated that in 2016 there was already a worldwide shortage of 13,600,000 professionals in the area of long-term care alone. Many of them are leaving because of the failure of the market and the state to provide well paid jobs with benefits in the care economy. A poll conducted by the largest long-term care union in the United States in 2015 found that half of nursing home workers were likely to leave the care economy in the next year because of poor wages. At the same time the demand for care services is predicted to increase dramatically over the next three decades as the population over the age of 60 rises to 2 billion. The number of people needing care is predicted to rise from 2.1 billion in 2015 to 2.3 billion in 2030. There are examples of regions around the world trying to address this situation. The California Department of Finance projects that by 2030 10.7 million, which accounts for 30 percent of all Californians, will be over the age 60. The proposed state budget for 2022–2023 includes historic investments of $1.7 billion over three years for care economy workforce development. This includes $350 million to recruit, train, and certify 25,000 new community health workers by 2025. But if we are to avert the global care crisis, we need to make the care economy an urgent priority worldwide, and publicly funded universal care services is the best response to this crisis.

Publicly Funded Universal Care Services: How Does It Work?

One way to approach publicly funded universal care services is to estimate the average amount of high-quality care each person needs as a child and as an adult who might be sick or elderly and then compute the cost of providing that care with well compensated, well-trained care providers. This amount is then allocated to each person to be spent on whoever ends up providing that care. For example, let's assume that a one-year-old child needs a certain number of hours of care. Some of these hours of care might be provided by the family and some of these hours might be provided by a day care provider. The amount allocated to this child would then be distributed between the family and the day care provider. All providers, whether they are family members, private care providers, public care providers, or community care providers would be well compensated, regulated, and trained to provide high-quality care. Different countries have been experimenting with different models of how to operationalize this basic principle. In this section we will briefly describe some of these models. Ultimately each community will have to identify for themselves the care provision model that works best within their cultural, social, and historical context. Care workers and care recipients need to recognize their common interests where good working conditions for care workers leads to good quality care for care recipients. It is imperative that both groups are included in the discussion and decision-making processes with regard to the regulation, training, and provision of care work. It is also important for formal sector care workers and informal sector care workers to form coalitions so that they are not pitted against each other but instead are able to work together to improve working and caring conditions for all care workers.

National Provision of Care Services

Globally, most low and middle-income countries do not have access to universal high-quality childcare services. Only 18.3% of children under the age of three enroll in early childhood education services. Long-term care services for those with disabilities are even less prevalent, ranging from 9% in Asia to 90% in Europe (ILO, 2018). Having said that, there have been some encouraging recent examples of countries with ambitious plans for providing comprehensive care services at a national level (UN Women, 2018b). Uruguay's Comprehensive National Care System (SNIC) instituted in 2015 is one such example. This system is based on the legal recognition that all children, older persons, and people with disabilities are entitled to care services, and it challenges the gendered nature of caregiving. A Care Advisory Committee was set up to bring together unions, private care providers, community organizations, and academics to guide the implementation of this program. The program provides a wide range of childcare centers, care spaces in study centers, care community houses, long-stay centers, personal carers, and teleassistance for older people and people with disabilities. The program also provides training for care providers to ensure quality of services offered. It includes expanded paid parental leave and a reduction in working hours for both parents until the child is six months old. It also includes initiatives to educate and encourage men to participate in care work. Mexico, Chile, Colombia, El Salvador, and the Dominican Republic are in the process of developing their own national care programs.

Another example is Ecuador's Public Policy for Comprehensive Child Support that is based on public childcare centers called Good Life Child centers. As a result of this effort, the percentage of children between 0 and 3 years of age who attend some type of childcare center has increased sixfold over the last 10 years. Cuba's preschool program enrolls over 99% of children between 0 and 6 years of age. Their program includes Children's Circles, created in 1961, which provides a comprehensive child development program. They also have an Educate Your Child program that encourages families to participate in child development activities with their children at home.

In 2021, Canada announced its plan to create a nationwide universal childcare system that will make childcare more affordable for Canadians (Lum, 2021). It is estimated that an investment of CA$30 billion over the next five years will create 300,000 new jobs over the next decade. These new jobs will generate tax revenue between CA$17 billion and CA$29 billion each year. They have also invested in long-term care services, although not at the same scale.

Employment Related Benefits

Another way to provide families with the option of participating in care work includes parental and family paid and unpaid leaves and flex work arrangements. Many countries around the world have leaves of this sort, but they vary in length and coverage. According to the ILO (2018) only 42% of countries have parental leave policies that meet the ILO standards for maternity leave, and 39% of countries have no paternity leave policies. For example, Jamaica provides eight weeks of maternity leave, whereas countries like Cuba, Paraguay, Chile, and Venezuela provide between 18 to 26 weeks of maternity leave. But in almost all these countries, paid paternity leave is rare and is of much shorter duration. For example, Venezuela and Paraguay provide 14 days of paternity leave. Leave to take care of sick or elderly family members is even less prevalent with only 29% of countries offering this kind of leave. Italy offers the most generous paid leave at full replacement for a period of two years. Most other countries in Europe offer shorter term leaves at partial replacement. The United States offers unpaid leave in the form of Family Medical Leave (FMLA). Although people that have jobs that offer paid sick leave can combine it with FMLA to get paid family medical leave. Social protection is usually available to those in formal employment, whereas most women work in the informal sector. As a result, about 60% of women, mostly in the informal sector, do not have access to any kind of leave. This has raised the question of whether we should have a global fund for social protection for all.

Nordic countries have been in the forefront of care policies that are coordinated to maximize coverage. For example, in Norway and Sweden there is a one month overlap between the end of paid parental leave and the start of eligibility for early childhood education services. They also offer some of the best coverage for long-term care for the elderly and persons with disabilities. Flex work arrangements were offered in many of the Nordic countries long before the pandemic. The pandemic has facilitated the development of flexible work arrangements, and it is possible that many workplaces might continue to offer telework options to their employees based on the nature of the work.

Cash Allowances/Benefits for Children

One of the ways of compensating and recognizing care work is by providing cash transfers/vouchers to families. More than two-thirds of countries have some version of a cash transfer. It has taken different forms in different countries with many conditions attached, which can end up privileging certain types of family and care arrangements. In France and Belgium, families are given vouchers they can use to purchase care services. The child support grant provided in South Africa is an example of trying to be neutral across different types of families by attaching the grant to the child and is paid to the primary caretaker of the child.

Community-Based Care Providers and Cooperatives

There are many examples of community organizations providing care in order to meet the needs of their communities. For example, Community Assistants is a home care program for the elderly in Chile. It helps with home care and companionship, administration of medications, and domestic tasks as needed by the elderly in their community. Another possibility is carepooling, similar to carpooling (Himmelweit, 2005). These are examples of women coming together and creating communal kitchens and community childcare, especially during times of crisis when the state has simply abdicated their responsibility for providing care. In Peru, mothers came together to collectively care for their children and provide them with sustenance (Blondet, 2002). In many countries the model of publicly funded community care services is the future of accountable and quality care provision.

Cooperatives have also played a role in providing care services for its members. For example, Asmare Waste Pickers Cooperative in Brazil worked with local government to fund community childcare centers that brought together multiple stakeholders, including local government, informal labor market workers, and childcare service providers to provide care for the children of waste pickers so that they can do a full day's work and their children receive good quality care. It also generates jobs for childcare workers. UPAVIM Cooperative of handicraft workers in Guatemala has a similar initiative where they manage a childcare center for their members. Another example is the Sangini Child Care workers' Cooperative in India, an initiative of the Self Employed Women's Association (SEWA) representing 1.5 million women workers in the informal economy, including agricultural workers, home-based workers, domestic workers, street vendors, and waste pickers. Sangini offers childcare services to its members through a shared stakeholder model that allows for parents of children, childcare workers, and local governments to work together to meet the needs of this community. They also offer opportunities for workers to receive training and employment in the center, which provides other health services in addition to childcare services (ILO/WIEGO 2018).

Reduction in Paid Work Hours

One collective solution might be to reduce paid work hours so we have more time to spend on caregiving and community service. This has benefits for climate change as this leads to reduction in consumption of goods and services and leads to greater well-being by encouraging social interaction and better health outcomes. It could also generate more jobs and lead to better quality care. This option will be further discussed in the next chapter.

How Do We Fund Universal Public Provision of Care Services?

Our broadest aspiration must be to go beyond GDP growth to include improvements in the health and well-being of all members of society, including present and future generations. Caring for human beings is the most direct way to achieve that aspiration. Everyone has the right to receive care, and investing in universal public provision of care services is the best way to reduce inequalities (including intergenerational inequalities) and improve everyone's life opportunities. We can learn from the experiences of countries that have made this commitment already, and I am sure that as more communities become involved in this effort, we will generate more innovative ideas of how to make this happen. Not only do I fully believe that it is possible to make this happen, I believe we can't afford to not make it happen.

Investing in the care economy is an investment in infrastructure because it generates jobs and tax revenue. According to the ILO (2018), investing in the care economy in a way that provides high quality care by well-paid care providers will require doubling the global investment we currently make in the care economy. This investment will result in 269 million new jobs. In a study of European countries, British economists Jerome De Henau and Susan Himmelweit (2020) found that investing in care results in more employment generation than investing in construction. Between a third to three-fifths of this investment in care is recouped through additional tax revenues from the new jobs created. Using this methodology, the corresponding estimate for Uruguay suggests that more than half of the investment would be recouped through tax revenues. We must rethink the concept of efficiency and productivity as cutting costs and increasing output per unit of labor input. In the care economy, increasing the number of people cared for by one care provider will only lower the quality of care. Instead, we need to think about higher wages leading to higher quality care. Funding high quality care will necessarily lead to the creation of more well-paid stable jobs in the care economy, which will help solve the jobs crisis. These new jobs will offer services that have a much smaller carbon footprint than the consumption of other types of goods and services. It will lead to higher well-being since caring for others and being cared for increases our social interaction, reduces anxiety, and improves health outcomes for all. Another way to link the climate crisis to the care crisis and the jobs crisis is to reallocate fossil fuel subsidies toward creating more jobs in the care economy and investing in the development of greener energies. Taxes on carbon and pollution will help shift consumption from high carbon footprint activities to low carbon footprint activities.

The initial investment for the universal public provision of care services plan can come from a variety of sources. Given the extreme inequality in the distribution of wealth and income, which has been further exacerbated by the pandemic, one source of revenue could be progressive taxation to ensure that the wealthiest people, corporations, and countries contribute the most to the recovery plan. We know that the bottom 50% of the global population owned less than 1% of all wealth in 2018, whereas the top 1% alone held almost half of it. We also know that in 2020, the combined earnings of workers around the world fell by US$3.7 trillion, while global billionaire wealth increased by US$3.9 trillion. A wealth tax on global billionaire wealth alone might be one way to help fund the plan. Another way might be the idea of a minimum global corporate tax rate that would ensure that corporations could not avoid it by moving their funds overseas to tax havens. Closing tax loopholes and stopping tax evasion might be another way to generate funds. It is estimated that US$7 trillion of the world's private wealth is funneled to offshore accounts not subject to taxation.

We also need to think about global redistribution of resources to correct massive inequalities in global access to resources. We need to change the global multilateral systems such as the IMF and credit rating agencies to allow for more diversity of approaches that matches the lived experiences of different countries. Credit rating agencies should operate more like public utilities, which allows for debt restructuring based on environmental sustainability, gender just outcomes, and reduction in inequalities. It also needs to include debt relief for countries hardest hit by the pandemic. At the other end, we must address tax evasion and progressive taxation for those who benefited the most from the pandemic. We need to prevent the inevitable austerity measures that come with debt restructuring by the IMF. Macroeconomic policies have typically focused on the market and the state and ignored the household and non-state non-market actors, most of who are women and most affected by austerity measures.

What Can I Do to Support This Effort?

All of these ideas will require campaigns to educate and to open minds and open hearts with regard to care work. We need to become aware of our interdependence and acknowledge and honor it instead of fearing it. We need to become aware of the inequalities that exist in the care economy and be motivated by compassion to do something about it, not only in our own communities but also globally, as we expand our definition of family to include the global community. We can look around at the people who are in our lives and reach out and share these insights with them to help them become aware and to learn from their lived experiences. We can express these ideas in songs or stories or poetry or art. Care work is everyone's collective responsibility, and many actions can be taken to move us in the direction of a more just and compassionate world. We can collaborate with and encourage men to take greater responsibility for care work in the household. Some examples of awareness campaigns include that of the Gregoria Apaza Center for the Promotion of Women, which used the slogan *Share the housework and enjoy the World Cup together d*uring the 2018 World Cup to raise awareness about the unequal care work distribution between men and women. Another example is the active fatherhood campaign launched by the Chile Grows with You initiative. If we employ domestic workers in our homes, we can provide them with paid leave and flexible hours so they can provide care to their loved ones when they need it. We can educate and encourage corporations to provide paid leave, flexible work arrangements, and care services when possible. We can encourage and support community organizations and unions to work together to demand benefits and fair compensation for all recipients and providers of care. We can educate, encourage, and support our local, state, and national governments to implement and fund universal high quality care services for all. We can participate in defining and choosing the best model for universal provision of care services within our own communities in an equitable way so that all voices are included and heard. We can encourage global multilateral entities to provide debt relief to our sisters and brothers in other countries. These are just some of the ways in which we can all participate and work together to bring about change. I hope that after reading this chapter you are motivated to develop your own action plans for change.

Key Takeaways

Below are the key ideas to take away from this chapter:

- Care work is required at those times in our lives when we have limited ability to take care of ourselves, and we have to depend on other human beings for care. It can be paid or unpaid and is typically provided by family members, by the state, by private care providers, or by community organizations. Most care—whether paid or unpaid—is provided by women.
- Unequal participation by women in unpaid care work results in unequal outcomes in the labor market. Unless we address inequalities in unpaid care work, we will not be able to achieve gender equality in other areas.
- Most paid care providers in the market are unregulated low-cost, low-wage care facilities that hire predominantly women from marginalized groups and immigrant women in the informal labor market. The paid and unpaid care economy is also plagued with the cost disease. There is no way to improve productivity in this kind of work without reducing the quality of care.
- Care work is one of the most direct ways in which we contribute to the survival, sustenance and flourishing of life. Receiving and providing high-quality care when we need it the most is the essence of building a more compassionate world.
- Inequalities in the care economy create and perpetuate inequalities in all other areas, making this a fundamental social justice issue that must be addressed if we want to create a more just and compassionate world.
- There is a looming global care crisis which necessitates making the care economy an urgent priority worldwide, and publicly funded universal care services is the best response to this crisis.
- Investing in the care economy is an investment in infrastructure because it generates jobs and tax revenue. Funding high-quality care will necessarily lead to the creation of more well-paid stable jobs in the care economy, which will help solve the jobs crisis. It will lead to higher well-being since caring for others and being cared for increases our social interaction, reduces anxiety, and improves health outcomes for all.

Comprehension Questions

Directions: Use what you have learned in this chapter to help you respond to the questions below:

1. What is the relationship between paid and unpaid care work?
2. What are the inequities in the care economy? How do these lead to unequal outcomes in the labor market?
3. What are the most significant factors that have led to the global care crisis? Why has the market been unable to provide high quality care to those who need it?
4. Why do we need publicly funded universal care services for all? How will it lead to greater well-being?
5. How do we fund universal publicly funded care services for all?

References

Blondet, C. (2002). The "devil's deal": Women's political participation and authoritarianism in Peru. In M. Molyneux, & S. Razavi (Eds.). *Gender Justice, Development and Rights*. Oxford University Press.

Chang E., & Levy B. (2021). High prevalence of elder abuse during the COVID-19 pandemic: Risk and resilience factors. *The American Journal of Geriatric Psychiatry,* 29(11), 1152–1159.

De Henau, J., Budlender, D., & Filgueira F. (2019). Investing in free universal childcare in South Africa, Turkey and Uruguay: A comparative analysis of costs, short-term employment effects and fiscal revenue. UN Women Discussion Paper No. 28. United Nations Entity for Gender Equality and the Empowerment of Women (UN Women), New York.

De Henau, J., & Himmelweit, S. (2020). Stimulating OECD economies post-Covid by investing in care. *IKD Working Paper No. 85. Innovation Knowledge and Development Research Centre,* The Open University, Milton Keynes, UK.

Elson, D. (2017). Recognize, reduce and redistribute unpaid care work: How to close the gender gap. *New Labour Forum, 26*(2), 52–61.

Folbre, N. (2006). Demanding quality: Worker/consumer coalitions and "high road" strategies in the care sector. *Politics and Society,* 34(1), 11–31.

Folbre, N., & Nelson, J. (2000). For love or money—or both? *Journal of Economic Perspectives,* 14(4), 123–140.

Gilbert, P. (2015). The evolution and social dynamics of compassion. *Social and Personality Psychology Compass,* 9(6), 239–254.

Helliwell, J. F., Aknin, L. B., Shiplett, H., Huang, H., & Wang, S. (2018). Social capital and prosocial behavior as sources of well-being. In E. Diener, S. Oishi, & L. Tay (Eds.), *Handbook of Well-Being*. Salt Lake City, UT: DEF Publishers.

Helliwell, J., Huang, H., Wang, S., & Norton, M. (2021). World happiness, trust and deaths under COVID 19. In *World Happiness Report 2021* (chapter 2).

Himmelweit, S. (2005). Can we afford (not) to care: Prospects and policy. GeNet Working Paper No. 11. Gender Equality Network, Economic and Social Research Council, Cambridge.

ILO (2018). Care Work and Care Jobs: For the Future of Decent Work. ILO: Geneva.

ILO/WIEGO (2018). *Cooperatives Meeting Informal Economy Workers' Childcare Needs—A Joint ILO and WIEGO Initiative.*

Kemeny, M., Foltz, C., Cavanagh, J., Cullen, M., Giese-Davis, J., Jennings, P., & Ekman, P. (2012). Contemplative/emotion training reduces negative emotional behavior and promotes prosocial responses. *Emotion, 12*(2), 338–350.

Leiberg S., Klimecki O., & Singer T. (2011). Short-term compassion training increases prosocial behavior in a newly developed prosocial game. *PLoS ONE* 6(3), 17798.

Lum, Z. (2021, April 29). What the budget means for Canadian women. *Chatelaine.*

MenCare. (2017). Estado de la paternidad en América Latina y el Caribe.

Razavi, S. (2007). *The political and social economy of care in a development context; Conceptual issues, research questions and policy options.* Gender and Development Programme Paper 3. Geneva: UNRISD.

UN Women (2020). *Macroeconomic policies for the feminist plan on sustainability and social justice.* Expert Group Meeting Report, Research and Data Section.

_____. 2018b. Recognition, redistribution and reduction of unpaid care work: Inspiring practices in Latin America and the Caribbean. Panama City, Panama: UN Women.

_____. 2020b. Whose time to care? Unpaid care and domestic work during COVID-19. UN Women, New York.

Weng, H., Fox, A., & Shackman, A. (2013). Compassion training alters altruism and neural responses to suffering. *Psychological Science,* 24(7), 1171–1180.

Yon Y., Mikton C., Gassoumis Z., & Wilber K. (2017). Elder abuse prevalence in community settings: a systematic review and meta-analysis. *Lancet Global Health,* 5(2), 147–156.

Yon Y., Ramiro-Gonzalez M., Mikton C., Huber M., & Sethi D. (2018). The prevalence of elder abuse in institutional settings: A systematic review and meta-analysis. *European Journal of Public Health,* 29(1), 58–67.

Chapter 8

Gender Justice and Sustainability

> We are the guardians of the territories, of the rivers, of the continuity of life. We understand the cycles of the moon, the spirituality of grandmothers, and the secrets of all the rituals of our communities. (So) when a corporation comes in and tries to destroy that social fabric and symbols of the community, the damage done is very deep. We are there to prevent this. Women defenders are making a lot of contributions and often they are not recognized.
>
> —Ana Maria Hernandez, land defender and director of grantee partner Consortio Oaxaca, a coalition of feminist activists in Mexico

From Local Stories to Global Visions

1n 1993 Berta Caceres, an Indigenous Lenca woman from Honduras, co-founded the Consejo Cívico de Organizaciones Populares y Indígenas de Honduras (Civic Council of Popular and Indigenous Organizations of Honduras, COPINH). COPINH has protested and been successful in stopping several logging projects and hydroelectric dams that have displaced indigenous peoples, including the dam over the Gualcarque River, which is sacred for the Lenca people. This dam was approved even though it was not in compliance with national and international environmental and community agreements. In 2016, Roberto David Castillo, the head of this dam, hired a hitman to assassinate Berta, two days before her 45th birthday. After a long struggle for justice, Castillo was finally convicted for Berta's murder in July 2021. Berta Caceres will always be remembered as a fearless advocate for the rights of indigenous peoples. She was also a LGBTQ campaigner, human rights activist, and an environmentalist.

Invitation to reflect: Take a moment to reflect on the courage that it took for Berta to stand up against powerful corporations that were destroying the environment and violating the rights of indigenous peoples.

Introduction

In chapter 7, we started the work of visioning and reimagining another path forward that will take us toward a more just and compassionate world. We looked back at the lessons we have learned from earlier chapters and used them as the foundation for a new vision. We focused on the care crisis that the pandemic has accelerated and discussed ways in which the care economy must be valued and funded to create the conditions for a just and compassionate recovery. In this chapter we will continue the work of developing a new vision by examining the interconnections between environmental crises and gender justice. We will consider ways in which we can envision and advocate for a more just and sustainable future.

As mentioned earlier, the unprecedented upheaval in our economic and social structures over the last three years has provided us with an opportunity and necessity to envision a different path forward that addresses the triple crises of job loss, climate change, and a fractured care economy. The recovery process must provide for the survival, sustenance, and flourishing of life. The current global economy relies on the exploitation of the environment, similar to the exploitation of women within the care economy, assuming that these resources are costless and limitless. The impact of overexploitation and overconsumption of natural resources falls disproportionately on marginalized groups, especially women living in low-income countries who contribute least to the overconsumption.

The feminist definition of development recognizes that we need to be better stewards of our natural resources and make choices that put the well-being of future generations and the long-term sustainability of our practices at the top of our priorities. This plan calls for transformative change by focusing on the synergies between sustainability and gender justice and putting care for all people and care for the planet front and center—creating decent jobs in green sectors and in the care economy and supporting sustainable agricultural practices to provide food security for all. A compassionate approach demands that everyone is included and everyone belongs.

What Is the Global Environmental Crisis?

The **global environmental crisis we face is defined as the growing inability of the planet's ecosystems to sustain life of current and future generations.** The main elements of this crisis include climate change, depletion of the ozone layer, degradation of air, water, and land quality, deforestation, and loss of biodiversity. Climate change is one of the most significant elements of the environmental crisis. According to the United Nations, **climate change refers to long-term shifts in temperatures and weather patterns. These shifts may be natural, such as through variations in the solar cycle. But since the 1800s, human activities have been the main driver of climate change, primarily due to burning fossil fuels like coal, oil, and gas.** The idea of planetary boundaries is another key concept that earth system scientists have brought to the table. These scientists argue that the unsustainable patterns of consumption and production over the last couple of centuries have propelled us into the Anthropocene era where human activities are the main drivers of earth system processes. Simply put, we are using the equivalent of 1.6 Earth systems to maintain our current consumption and production patterns. If we continually transgress the boundaries within which human life is possible on this planet, we will be driven irrevocably into the next phase of planetary history where the survival of millions of species—including the human species—is at risk.

Overconsumption of resources (assuming that resources are limitless) has led to overexploitation of natural resources, loss of biodiversity, and pollution of our oceans, air, and rivers. The resulting carbon emissions are leading to melting polar caps, rising water levels and flooding, and heat waves and droughts.

Invitation to reflect: Take a moment to reflect on changes in weather patterns that you have experienced in the last several years. How did they affect your life?

High income countries are the largest emitters with the top 10 countries accounting for more than 68% of global emissions. Low-income countries that emit the least are the ones who are affected the most and the least able to withstand the adverse impacts of climate change. For example, India emits less than 3% of world's greenhouse gases and yet faces unprecedented heat waves such as the most recent one in 2022 in northern India and Pakistan with temperatures rising above 110 degrees Fahrenheit. Being a low-income country, less than 10% of Indians have access to air-conditioning (or even electricity), which makes it harder for them to deal with the unbearable heat. Climate change also affects food crops leading to drought and famine in some of the poorest areas in the world such as West Africa, whose people have contributed the least to climate change. The fossil fuel industry also affects the composition of the soil because of unsustainable mining practices and pollution due to oil spills.

Carbon emissions are now 62% higher than they were in 1990 when global climate negotiations began in earnest. As per the Paris Agreement on Climate Change (UNFCCC, 2015), we need to make significant reductions in global emissions in order to stay well below global temperature increases of 2 degrees centigrade and closer to 1.5 degrees. If we don't achieve these targets, then it is estimated that we will lose one million species to extinction and areas where billions of humans live today will become unlivable. Many scientists argue that the habitat loss and deforestation due to this current model of economic growth led to COVID -19, which they argue is one of many pandemics that we can expect to face over the next few decades (Gupta et al, 2021; Chakraborty & Maity, 2020).

On the production side, reducing carbon emissions on this scale is only possible with the phasing out of fossil fuels, which means that not only do we need to immediately stop investing in fossil fuels, we also need to halt most existing fossil fuel projects. However, we have yet to see any significant action in this direction. Instead, we continue to invest in fossil fuel projects. Between 2016 and 2019 at least $2.7 trillion was lent to fossil fuel firms by the banking sector (Rainforest Action Network, 2020). In the absence of the pandemic, we were set to exceed our fossil fuel production by 50% to 120% (Stockholm Environment Institute (SEI), 2019). The pandemic and the accompanying recession did temporarily disrupt consumption patterns in 2020, which led to a sudden immediate drop in carbon emissions. It was short-lived, and once the economy started opening up, consumption patterns returned to pre-pandemic levels. In addition, the drop in consumption in 2020 was not equally distributed as the wealthiest individuals felt the least impact (Kommenda, 2021). Most countries are gearing up to go back to "business as usual," which is hugely problematic in the fossil fuel industry.

Invitation to reflect: Take a moment to reflect on your own consumption of fossil fuels. What prevents you from reducing your consumption of fossil fuels? Did the experience of the pandemic teach us lessons about fossil fuel consumption that we can use moving forward?

"Business as usual" would take us in the opposite direction of the Paris agreement on climate change. According to the 2021 Production Gap Report (Stockholm Environment Institute (SEI), 2021), "Governments' production plans and projections would lead to around 240% more coal, 57% more oil, and 71% more gas than would be consistent with limiting global warming to 1.5°C."

The phasing out of fossil fuels will create trillions of dollars of *stranded assets* in the fossil fuel industry, which are defined as assets that have experienced a sudden drop in value or have become liabilities (Rempell & Gupta, 2021). Those who hold these assets, not surprisingly, are pushing hard to prevent the stranding of their assets by continuing to increase the production and consumption of fossil fuels. The pandemic, which abruptly stranded some of these assets due to massive drops in fossil fuel consumption, might have eased our way to a stranding of assets as we accelerate the phaseout of fossil fuels. In other words, let us not go back to business as usual. Let us use this opportunity to chart a new course that is more sustainable and just. Rempell & Gupta (2021) outlined four possible recovery scenarios, only one of which satisfies social, economic, and ecological inclusiveness. The first scenario would prioritize recovery in profits and recovery in returns to investment of the wealthy (back to business as usual). This scenario would move us further away from reducing global temperature changes by less than two degrees. It would further increase social and economic inequalities and put us on a downward spiral, which eventually would exclude all of us from the planet. Early evidence indicates that most countries are choosing this scenario. It is imperative that we do a U-turn and choose the sustainable and just path before it is too late. It is also important to recognize that the impact of these stranded assets is also felt by human beings whose livelihoods depend upon the fossil fuel industry. To ensure a just and inclusive transition we need to ensure that they have the opportunity to retrain and have access to jobs in the new green economy.

Why Is the Environmental Crisis a Social Justice Issue?

Women, especially poor and indigenous women in rural areas, are disproportionately affected by climate change because of their greater reliance on natural resources and because of their unequal access to it. Women who are mostly responsible for subsistence agriculture and for daily household tasks of fetching water, collecting firewood, or foraging for food are disproportionately affected by the impact of climate change on soil conditions, water sources, and forests. Not only do they experience an increase in time spent on these activities, but they also face food and income insecurity for themselves and their families. According to Erman et al. (2021), women are disproportionately affected by floods, fires, droughts, and other natural disasters. The disasters themselves are neutral, but when placed within the context of structural gender inequalities, they not only affect women's abilities to respond, withstand, and recover from disasters, but they also further exacerbate existing inequalities in terms of life expectancy, gender violence, health, education, unemployment, and loss of assets.

Studies have shown that the impact of natural disasters on loss of life depends upon several factors. In high-income countries such as in Europe and the United States, men account for 70% of deaths due to flooding because they are more likely to be at the forefront of rescue efforts. In low-income countries, however, women are more likely to die from disasters because of lack of access to information, mobility, and safe shelters. For example, women were three to five times more likely to die during the cyclone in Bangladesh in 1991 (Ikeda, 1995). Women are also much more likely to experience post-traumatic stress and anxiety after natural disasters due to lack of social support structures, greater perception of threat, and the nature of the trauma, which often includes sexual violence. Disasters can often precipitate violence, and women and children are more likely to bear the brunt of it. Studies have shown that from earthquakes in Haiti (Weitzman & Behrman, 2016) and droughts in Tanzania (Abiona & Foureaux Koppensteiner, 2018) to hurricanes in the United States (Harville et al., 2011), disasters lead to higher rates of sexual violence against women from strangers and intimate partners.

Girl children are more likely to be kept home from school or receive less nutrition or health care if resources are scarce after a disaster hits and parents have to make choices about whom to feed and whom to send to school. If parents die due to a disaster this increases the likelihood of child marriages for girls, but not for boys. For example, after the tsunami in Sumatra in 2004, girls were 62% more likely to be married versus boys were 7% less likely to be married. Disasters can also lead to changes in consumption patterns, especially for women and girls who are more likely to go hungry when resources are scarce. For example, women were 1.6 times more likely to be hungry post disaster in Bangladesh (Shoji, 2010), reflecting gendered power differentials that translate to poorer health outcomes for women in the long run.

Burning of fossil fuels and biomass are the chief causes of airborne pollution. Pollution of our natural resources is the largest environmental cause of disease and premature morbidity, disproportionately affecting women and marginalized communities globally. In 2015, pollution led to 9 million premature deaths, 92% of which happened in low and middle-income countries (UN Environment, 2019). Women and children are particularly vulnerable. Women's access to reproductive health services are also often disrupted by disasters, which could lead to unplanned pregnancies.

In low-income countries women are responsible for most subsistence farming, and they tend to be far worse off during floods or droughts because they have less access to capital, technology, and rescue efforts. They are also overburdened by unpaid care responsibilities that arise during the aftermath of a disaster. Men often migrate to other areas in search of employment while women are often left to take care of the children, the sick, and elderly. Disasters also lead to higher unemployment rates among women than men. For example, in the Colombian Caribbean region, women were 3% more likely than men to experience unemployment due to floods (Acevedo, 2014). Women also find it harder to get re-employed after disasters. Men are more likely to find employment in post-disaster construction activities than women, due to high levels of occupational segregation in those industries. For example, a year after Hurricane Katrina hit New Orleans, Louisiana, in 2005, women's earnings were 7% lower than before the disaster as compared to men whose earnings were 23% higher (Peek & Fothergill, 2008).

Female-headed households are more likely to reside in high hazard areas, which means that they are disproportionately affected by natural disasters. For example, female-headed households in Dar es Salaam, Tanzania were more likely to experience flooding (Erman et al., 2019). Globally, women own only 20% of all land resources, which means that they have less access to capital and are more likely to be house insecure, especially after a disaster. As mentioned earlier, women—especially poor and indigenous women of color—are much more likely to be in the informal labor market without access to any social protections, which makes them particularly vulnerable when a disaster occurs. Due to lack of access to the banking system, many women keep their assets in the home, which are more likely to be destroyed during natural disasters. They are also more likely to be sold to help cope with the post disaster drop in resources. For example, in Uganda, women's assets drop after a drought, but men's assets remain unchanged (Quisumbing et al., 2018). The fact that the environmental crisis has a disproportionate impact on women and other marginalized communities makes it a social justice issue that must be central to solving the environmental crisis.

History of Environmental Policy and Gender Outcomes

Eco-feminist Vandana Shiva's pioneering work (1988) brought attention to the exploitation of women and nature as cornerstones of colonization and capitalist profit-making processes in the last few centuries. Colonial environmental practices that emerged in the early 20th century were largely driven by moral and paternalistic narratives about preserving the "pristine wilderness" of the lands they had colonized. Nature preserves were created and other policies implemented in the name of protecting the land from the local people, who were labelled as destroyers of the environment (Fairhead & Leach, 1996). This argument was used to justify large-scale displacement of local peoples from their lands, the gendered impact of which was largely ignored by the colonizers. This behavior and exploitative process continues into the present day where the search for alternative sources of energy has led to the funding of large-scale hydroelectric power plants without any attention paid to the displacement and loss of livelihoods of local communities (Mehta, 2009). Going down this path creates a narrative where people's livelihoods are at odds with the environment. We are forced into a false choice between poverty and environmental degradation when in reality this approach creates both.

The environmental movement as a social movement gathered strength during the 1970s. In the global North, the environmental movement brought awareness to the impact of economic growth fueled by nonrenewable energy sources on pollution, resource depletion, habitat, and species loss.

Invitation to reflect: Take a moment to reflect on when and in what context you first heard about climate change and the environmental crisis. How did it make you feel? What was your reaction?

The fear of resources running out could have led to the curbing of unsustainable consumption and production behaviors, especially by those in the global North. Instead, the problem was framed as unsustainable population growth in the global South, leading to further control over women's bodies as policies were implemented to reduce fertility rates (Hartmann et al., 2015). Within a militaristic framework wherein most countries around the world spend more money on defense than investing in social services and the green economy, environmental degradation was and continues to be seen as a security threat. A rush to close borders and build walls to stem migration driven by climate change (and violence stemming from the same militarism) is often the response of countries of the global North to the environmental crisis. Environmental and social movements in the global South have focused more on the impact of economic and environmental policies on the livelihoods and rights of poor and indigenous communities. For example, the Chipko movement in India in

1974 was about resisting the cutting down of trees for industrial use to protect the livelihoods of local communities. Women played a major role in this movement since they were primarily responsible for collecting firewood and providing food for their families. Kenya's Green Belt Movement founded by Wangari Maathai in 1977 is another example of rural women protecting their livelihoods by planting trees.

By the 1980s, the WID (women in development) approach inspired by Boserup's work (as discussed in chapter 3) was increasingly informed by the central role women play in the management of the environment, giving rise to the WED (women, the environment and development) approach. This approach also highlighted the gendered impact of environmental degradation (Harcourt, 1994). While WED changed the ways that the World Bank and other global entities approached environmental projects, women often came to be seen as the saviors of the environment without questioning the disproportionate burden being placed on women to address these issues without remuneration. The WED approach overlapped with ecofeminism approaches that arose in the late 1980s and early 1990s as another strand of the nexus between gender and the environment. **While there are several variants of ecofeminism, most ecofeminists believe that women and nature share a common bond (Shiva, 1988). For the white male colonizer, the physical environment, people of color, and women have all been assumed to be part of nature to be controlled and exploited.** This assumption was used as a justification for the exploitation and extraction of surplus. According to this view, the liberation of all three is tied together in that one is not possible without the other.

In 1987, *Our Common Future,* the World Commission on Environment and Development report identified the economic, environmental, and social aspects of sustainable development, making the link between the environment and human well-being more explicit. In 1991, several NGOs working on different aspects of gender and sustainable development—such as the Women's Environment and Development Organization (WEDO)—came together to establish Women's Action Agenda 21, which led to the World Women's Congress for a Healthy Planet in Miami. The goal was to mainstream gender issues so that sustainable development without gender equity would be unthinkable. In 1992, the United Nations Conference on Environment and Development was held in Rio. It was the first intergovernmental summit where different approaches to sustainable development were discussed and argued. High level global conventions were launched to address key issues, such as climate change and biodiversity. While they recognized the global women's lobby, gender and sustainable livelihoods was not placed front and center. As a result, much of what followed did not lead to transformative change.

Feminist political ecology (FPE) and gender, environment, and development (GED) are other strands that gained momentum in the early 1990s. They look at the relationship between women and the environment as being embedded in dynamic social relations, which create power differentials based on multiple identities and relationships. For example, an indigenous woman living in a female-headed household in a rural area might have a very different relationship with the environment compared to that of a poor white woman living in a male-headed household in an urban area. The impact of environmental policies can also shape and be shaped by these intersecting power differentials caused by social relations.

Invitation to reflect: Take a moment to reflect on your relationship with the environment. To what extent do you think it is conditioned by your social identities and intersecting power differentials?

FPE also acknowledges multiple ways of knowing and challenges the power differentials inherent in knowledge production in general and knowledge about ecology in particular (Wright, 2010). For example, forest spaces are often used by different groups in different ways. Corporate interests might see forests as a source of lumber and profit. Poor women who live in or near forests see forests as a source of firewood, food, medicines, and crucial to the fertility of the soil on which they cultivate other crops. They might also see forests as sacred sites of worship. Men who live locally might see forests as a space for hunting and initiation rites. Forests have also been subject to changing policies by governmental agencies. They might see forests as tourism sites that will generate revenue for the state. More recently, forests—especially in the global South—have been seen as a way to offset carbon emissions by the global North. As a result, each group's relationship with the forest is embedded in complex social relationships, and the decision about which part of the forest is cleared and which part is conserved becomes one of contested power differentials. Leach et al. (2016) ask the question what is being sustained and for whom? Community-based joint forest management is one way to resolve these competing uses and impacts, but here too, women have not always been included in the decision-making processes. Bela Agarwal's (2010) recent study of community-based management of forests in Nepal and India found that in places where women have been included, the forests are shared more equally and the outcomes are more positive in terms of gender equality and ecological sustainability.

Coming to the present time, new feminist political ecology (NFPE) has added insights from a performative gender approach that recognizes the processes by which gender is constructed and reconstructed (Osborne & Segal, 1994). This approach also highlights the importance of embodied experience of environmental practices. NFPE has engaged with queer theory to challenge the binary construction of gender and heterosexism present in ecofeminist thought.

The 2012 United Nations Conference on Sustainable Development highlighted the importance of climate change, planetary boundaries, and the green economy. The earlier global compact around common but differentiated responsibility had fallen apart. The Green Economy Initiative, launched in 2008 by the United Nations Environment Programme (UNEP), identifies an economy as green if it is low carbon, resource efficient and socially inclusive. Green economies would have to transform their consumption and production patterns such that they are no longer dependent on nonrenewable energy sources and invest in alternative energy sources and sustainable agricultural practices (Jackson, 2009). They would maximize well-being versus economic growth, which would require investments in social services and the care economy as well as creation of well-paid jobs in these sectors. Gender equality was almost absent from the conversation even though gender justice is at the heart of climate change (Wichterich, 2012). Feminists (Schalatek, 2013) have critiqued the green economy approach as not going far enough to bring about transformative change. They want to see a gender equitable sustainable development framework, which puts gender equity at the center of the framework. By casting climate change as a universal global challenge we all face, we ignore the differential impact of climate change on women, especially poor and indigenous women. We also fail to acknowledge their agency and knowledge, for instance by not including a single woman on the advisory group on climate financing in 2010. Feminist visions often call for transformative change at all levels, which is more threatening to the status quo than making small changes on the margins. Raworth (2012) argues for a socially just space, which includes gender justice, within the planetary boundaries that we should aim to stay within as we develop global plans to address sustainable development. The sustainable development goals established in 2015 explicitly include gender equality as one of the 17 SDGs, which is a major step forward. However, it is also important to integrate gender equality with the other SDGs so that gender issues don't get siloed once again.

Gender Justice and Sustainability: Another Cornerstone of a Just and Compassionate World

According to Leach et al. (2016), "**Sustainable development is development that ensures human well-being, ecological integrity, gender equality and social justice, now and in the future.**" By making gender equality and social justice integral to the process of sustainable development we ensure that not just men and women have equal access, equal recognition, and equal decision-making power, but also the intersections of race, class, sexuality, gender identities, place, and other forms of marginalization are addressed. Leach et al. (2016) argue that sustainability and gender equality can reinforce each other by using a gendered pathways approach. As mentioned before, they ask the question sustainability of what and for whom? We need to include local and indigenous peoples and women who are most impacted by environmental degradation in the process of finding and funding equitable and sustainable solutions.

If the goal is food sustainability for all, then perhaps we need to form a rights-based approach that supports small-scale farmers to pursue ecologically sound cultivation, maintain soil fertility, and meet the food needs of their communities while respecting local and indigenous knowledge of ecological practices and local environmental conditions. It is important to acknowledge and respect women's contributions to food provision at the same time it is important to dismantle structures that have placed this burden unfairly on the shoulders of women and exploited their unpaid and underpaid labor. In other words, gender-just transitions to sustainability require that we don't place the burden of "saving the earth" on women, especially poor indigenous women of color. It is our shared and collective responsibility to live in harmony with and within our planetary boundaries. The state has an important role to play in holding private entities accountable to agreed-upon principles and regulations. They can also support small-scale farmers by facilitating flow of credit, transportation, seeds, ecologically sound technologies, and social protections in case of natural disasters. They can also ensure labor protections, safe working conditions, and property rights of poor and indigenous peoples. Social movements and community organizations also have a role to play in advocating and supporting these approaches, while at the same time resisting approaches that create and maintain structural inequalities.

The new feminist vision of post-COVID-19 recovery puts care for people and care for the planet front and center. The definition of the economy by feminist economists focuses on social provisioning, i.e., producing goods and services that are needed for all humans and other species to have equal opportunity to flourish in a way that uses resources without creating social and ecological debt. The wealthiest countries, corporations, and people need to reduce their consumption so we can invest in gender just transitions to sustainability. Easterlin's work (2003) within the well-being literature reminds us that after we reach a certain level of income then further increases in income and consumption do not lead to higher levels of well-being. Therefore, reducing the consumption of high-income countries is not likely to reduce well-being. If people can reduce their consumption of goods and services and instead spend time building strong social relationships, helping and caring for others, and focusing on their own health, they have a much better chance of experiencing sustained happiness. One proposal mentioned in chapter 6 was that a reduction in hours worked and an accompanying increase in hours spent with loved ones and hours spent on improving one's health might lead to greater well-being as well as reduce carbon emissions.

Invitation to reflect: Take a moment to reflect on one change that you can make to reduce your consumption of goods and services and instead focus on an activity that increases your well-being and is good for the environment.

We also need to focus on regeneration versus depletion of natural resources. For example, Bhutan is a carbon negative country. It has actually increased its forest cover over the last few decades at the same time that the rest of the world is experiencing deforestation. As mentioned in chapter 3, they have been able to accomplish this by adopting the concept of Gross National Happiness (GNH) versus Gross Domestic Product (GDP). The four pillars of GNH are equitable socioeconomic development, preservation of culture, conservation of the environment, and good governance. All their policies have to be in alignment with these four values. For example, they have a zero-homelessness policy, which ensures more equitable socioeconomic development and sustainable use of their land. They also have a tourism policy, which limits the number of tourists and automobiles to reduce the carbon footprint of tourism activities in their country.

Market-driven solutions, such as trading carbon permits, have not reduced carbon emissions. In fact, it has exacerbated inequalities as rich countries and corporations have displaced indigenous communities in their pursuit of large-scale renewable energy projects, such as palm oil plantations in Southeast Asia. In many cases the refusal to grant land rights to indigenous communities allows governments to classify the land as vacant and thereby open to sale and displacement of communities that have been stewards of that land for generations. It is critical that as we transition to renewable sources of energy, we include indigenous voices and concerns in the process to ensure that their rights and livelihoods are protected. Renewable energy projects can be sustainable and equitable by inviting indigenous peoples to work in collaboration with others to develop their own micro off-grid renewable energy systems. One example is the indigenous peoples of northern Luzon working with SIBAT, a nonprofit organization in the Philippines that brings renewable technology to rural areas (Thazin Aung, 2020).

As we build back our economies, we can choose to create decent, well-paid jobs in the green economy, those sectors that contribute to the sustenance and flourishing of life, those sectors that have a low or negative carbon footprint. One such sector is the care economy we discussed in chapter 7. Gender responsive agroecology and green energy are two other sectors that we should invest in. We need to ensure that these sectors allow for decentralized systems where women—especially poor and indigenous women—are able to participate in identifying the issues and creating the solutions. According to the UN Women (2021), extractive industries are responsible for 50% of carbon emissions and 80% of biodiversity loss. Therefore, we need to change the mix of industries. As we turn to renewable sources of energy, we should pay attention to the negative ecological impact they might have, such as mining the rare earth minerals required for batteries (Scholten et al., 2020).

How Do We Fund Gender-Just Transitions to Sustainability?

Those countries, corporations, and people who have historically contributed the most to carbon emissions and currently have the highest amount of wealth and consumption should be the ones who contribute the most to the effort. Economic growth in these economies has historically been based on the colonization of most countries in the global South, genocide of indigenous peoples, and enslavement of African peoples. This is their opportunity to pay back their social and ecological debt (Ciplet, 2017). Fossil fuel subsidies in place in over 40 countries total about $320 billion in 2019 and can be reallocated toward funding and incentivizing the provision of care services and technologies with a low carbon footprint, which contribute to the sustaining and flourishing of life and correct gender and other inequalities. The transition will require retraining laborers who are being let go from high carbon emissions jobs. It is imperative that women have equal access to the 24 million green jobs that will be created in the transition to sustainability. Climate finance needs to prioritize mitigation and gender responsive adaptation of the poorest countries that have been hit hardest by climate change. Volz et al. (2020) have argued for debt relief tied to green recovery commitments.

Partnerships and Collective Responsibility

It is critical that governments work in partnership with local and indigenous communities, NGOs, private industry, and women's organizations to find solutions that create sustainable livelihoods for all and challenge entrenched gendered inequities. Expanding access to clean renewable energy benefits everyone but has had a significantly greater impact on women. Community managed microgrids have been found to promote gender justice and be sustainable. For example, Afghanistan has used microgrids and solar energy to increase access to electricity from 28% in 2006 to 84% in 2016 (UN Women, 2019). Decentralized microgrid energy programs can also increase employment and entrepreneurship opportunities for women. For example, Solar Sister, a nonprofit organization, trained over 4,000 women to sell affordable solar-powered cookstoves in off-grid communities in Nigeria, Uganda, and United Republic of Tanzania (Solar Sister, 2018). The solutions are not the same everywhere, and it is important for each of us to work together to find local solutions that are inclusive and sustainable.

Invitation to reflect: Take a moment to reflect on how you might work with others in your community to reduce carbon emissions and create sustainable livelihoods for all, especially women.

The food sector is another high carbon emitting sector that needs to transition to more sustainable practices promoted by agroecology. These practices use natural synergies between plants and animals to create combinations of crops that promote soil health and biodiversity. Agroecology promotes partnerships between local and indigenous peoples, small farmers and local systems that do not require large capital outlays and costly inputs (Akram-Lodhi, 2021). It also improves nutrition of household farms, which reduces what has been mostly women's work in providing food for the family. It is also important to hold people/countries/corporations accountable for meeting the goals of gender just transitions to sustainable development. Social movements have often played a key role in resisting environmental degradation and violations of human rights. While they will continue to play that role, it is important for governmental and intergovernmental agencies to hold each other accountable and stay the course. It is encouraging that beginning in 2016, the International Criminal Court has recognized environmental crimes as part of its domain.

It is important to recognize that we are interdependent on each other and on our environment. Our best hope of fully experiencing our humanity is to care for each other and care for the environment that we live in, not out of fear but out of a need to celebrate our deep and necessary connectedness. We are like drops of water thinking that we are separate when in fact we are all part of the same ocean. Our fates are inextricably tied to each other and to the ocean that we are part of, whether we are aware of it or not. None of us is more or less important than the other, and we can thrive if and only if we all do. There are several studies available describing how we can make more sustainable choices and how we can support each other so that everyone has a chance to thrive. We just have to have the willingness to do it. Our resources may be limited, but our capacity for compassion is infinite—if only we choose to act on it.

Key Takeaways

Below are the key ideas to take away from this chapter:

- The global economy relies on the exploitation of the environment similar to the exploitation of women within the care economy, assuming that these resources are costless and limitless.
- If we continually transgress the boundaries within which human life is possible on this planet, the survival of millions of species—including the human species—is at risk.
- The impact of overexploitation and overconsumption of natural resources falls disproportionately on marginalized groups, especially women living in low-income countries who (ironically) contribute least to the overconsumption.
- The environmental movement as a social movement gathered strength during the 1970s. In the global North, the environmental movement brought awareness to the impact of economic growth fueled by nonrenewable energy sources—on pollution, resource depletion, habitat, and species loss.
- Environmental and social movements in the global South focused more on the impact of economic and environmental *policies* on the livelihoods and rights of poor and indigenous communities.
- By making gender equality and social justice integral to the process of sustainable development we ensure that not just men and women have equal access, equal recognition, and equal decision-making power, but also the intersections of race, class, sexuality, gender identities, place, and other forms of marginalization are addressed.
- The countries, corporations, and people that have historically contributed the most to carbon emissions and currently have the highest amount of wealth and consumption should be the ones who contribute most to the effort of mitigating the environmental crisis.

Comprehension Questions

Directions: Use what you have learned in this chapter to help you respond to the questions below:

1. How has the current economic model of overconsumption led to the environmental crisis?
2. Why is the environmental crisis a social justice issue?
3. How and why do we combine gender justice with sustainable development in our post COVID recovery plan?
4. How do we fund gender just transitions toward sustainability?

References

Abiona, O. & Foureaux Koppensteiner, M. (2018). *The Impact of Household Shocks on Domestic Violence: Evidence from Tanzania.* IZA Discussion Paper No. 11992. Institute for Labor Economics.

Acevedo, M. (2014). *The Effect of Extreme Hydro-Meteorological Events on Labor Market Outcomes: Evidence from the Colombian Caribbean.* Harvard Environmental Economics Research Seminar.

Agarwal, B. (2010). *Gender and Green Governance: The Political Economy of Women's Presence Within and Beyond Community Forestry.* Oxford University Press.

Akram-Lodhi, A. H. (2021). The ties that bind? Agroecology and the agrarian question in the twenty-first century. *The Journal of Peasant Studies,* 48(4), 687–714.

Chakroborty, I., & Maity, P. (2020). COVID-19 outbreak: Migration, effects on society, global environment and prevention. Science of the Total Environment, 728, 1–7. https://doi.org/10.1016/j.scitotenv.2020.138882.

Ciplet, D. (2017). Subverting the status quo? Climate debt, vulnerability and counter-hegemonic frame integration in United Nations climate politics: Framework for analysis. *Review of International Political Economy,* 24(6), 1052–1075.

Easterlin, R. (2003). Explaining happiness. *Proceedings of the National Academy of Sciences of the United States of America,* 100(19), 11176–11183.

Erman, A., De Vries Robbe, S., Browne, N., & Solis Uehara, C. (2021). *Gender Dimensions of Disaster Risk and Resilience.* Washington, DC: World Bank.

Erman, A., Tariverdi, M., Xiaomeng, M., Rose, C., Vincent, C., Malgioglio, S., Rentschler, J., Hallegatte, S., & Yoshida, N. (2019). *Wading out the Storm: The Role of Poverty in Exposure, Vulnerability and Resilience to Floods in Dar Es Salaam.* Washington, DC: World Bank.

Fairhead, J., & Leach, M. (1996). *Misreading the African Landscape: Society and Ecology in a Forest Savanna Mosaic.* Cambridge University Press.

Gupta, J., Bavinck, M., Ros-Tonen, M., Asubonteng, K., Bosch, H., van Ewijk, E., Hordijk, M., Van Leynseele, Y., Lopes Cardozo, M., Miedema, E., Pouw, N., Rammelt, C., Scholtens, J., Vegelin, C., & Verrest, H. (2021). COVID-19, poverty and inclusive development. World Development, 145.

Harcourt, W. (1994). Negotiating Positions in the Sustainable Development Debate: Situating the Feminist Perspective. In W. Harcourt (Eds.), *Feminist Perspectives on Sustainable Development* (pp.11–26). Zed Books.

Hartmann, B., Hendrixson, A., & Sasser, J. (2015). Population, sustainable development and gender equality. In M. Leach (Ed.), *Gender Equality and Sustainable Development* (pp. 56–81). Oxford and New York: Routledge.

Harville, E., Taylor, C., Tesfai, H., Xiong, X., & Buekens, P. (2011). Experience of Hurricane Katrina and reported intimate partner violence. *Journal of Interpersonal Violence,* 26(4), 833–845.

Ikeda, K. (1995). Gender differences in human loss and vulnerability in natural disasters: A case study from Bangladesh. *Indian Journal of Gender Studies,* 2(2), 171–193.

Jackson, T. (2009). *Prosperity Without Growth: Economics for a Finite Planet.* London: Earthscan/Routledge.

Kommenda, N. (2021, January 21). Wealthy UK flyers opt for private jets to evade COVID lockdowns. *The Guardian.*

Leach, M., Mehta, L., & Prabhakaran, P. (2016). *Gender Equality and Sustainable Development: A Pathways Approach.* UN Women Discussion Paper No. 13. United Nations Entity for Gender Equality and the Empowerment of Women (UN Women), New York.

Mehta, L. (Ed.). (2009). *Displaced by Development: Confronting Marginalisation and Gender Injustice.* New Delhi: Sage Publications.

Osborne, P., & Segal, L. (1994). Gender as performance: An interview with Judith Butler. *Radical Philosophy. 67,* 32–39.

Peek, L., & Fothergill, A. (2008). Displacement, gender, and the challenges of parenting after Hurricane Katrina. *National Women's Studies Association Journal,* 20(3), 69–105.

Quisumbing, A., Kumar, N., & Behrman, J. (2018). Do shocks affect men's and women's assets differently? Evidence from Bangladesh and Uganda. *Development Policy Review,* 36(1), 3–34.

Rainforest Action Network. (2020). *Banking on Climate Change.* San Francisco: RAN.

Raworth, K. (2012). *A Safe and Just Space for Humanity: Can We Live Within the Doughnut?* Oxfam Discussion Papers. Oxfam, Oxford.

Rempel, A. & Gupta, J. (2021). Fossil fuels, stranded assets and COVID-19: Imagining an inclusive & transformative recovery. World Development, 146, 1-12. https://doi.org/10.1016/j.worlddev.2021.105608

Schalatek, L. (2013). *The Post-2015 Framework: Merging Care and Green Economy Approaches to Finance Gender-Equitable Sustainable Development.* Berlin: Heinrich Boell Foundation.

Scholten, D., Bazilian, M., Overland, I., & Westphal, K. (2020). The geopolitics of renewables: New board, new game. *Energy Policy,* 138.

Shiva, V. (1988). *Staying Alive: Women, Ecology, and Development.* Zed Books.

Shoji, M. (2010). Does contingent repayment in microfinance help the poor during natural disasters? *Journal of Development Studies,* 46(2), 191–210.

Solar Sister. (2018). *What We Do*. https://solarsister.org/what-we-do/
Stockholm Environment Institute, IISD, ODI, Climate Analytics, CICERO, UNEP. (2019). *The production gap: The discrepancy between countries' planned fossil fuel production and global production levels consistent with limiting warming to 1.5C or 2C*. Stockholm: Stockholm Environment Institute.
________. (2021). *The Production Gap Report*. Stockholm: Stockholm Environment Institute.
Thazin Aung, M. (2020, June 4). A just transition to renewables must recognize the rights of Indigenous Peoples. Stockholm Environment Institute Perspectives. https://www.sei.org/perspectives/a-just-transition-to-renewables-must-recognize-the-rights-of-indigenous-peoples/
UN Environment. (2019). Global Environment Outlook—GEO-6: Healthy Planet, Healthy People. Nairobi.
UNFCCC (United Nations Framework Convention on Climate Change). (2015). Adoption of the Paris Agreement. Conference of the Parties 21st Session. Paris.
UN Women. (2019). World survey on the role of women in development 2019: Why addressing women's income and time poverty matters for sustainable development. New York: UN Women.
UN Women. (2021). Beyond Covid-19: A feminist plan for sustainability and social justice. Research and Data Section, UN Women.
Volz, U., Akhtar, S., Gallagher, K., Griffith-Jones, S., & Haas, J. (2020). *Debt relief for a green and inclusive recovery: A proposal*. Heinrich Boll Stiftung; Global Development Policy Center, Boston University, Boston, MA; and Centre for Sustainable Finance, SOAS, London.
Weitzman, A., & Behrman, J. (2016). Disaster, disruption to family life, and intimate partner violence: The case of the 2010 earthquake in Haiti. *Sociological Science*, 3, 167–189.
Wichterich, C. (2012). The future we want: A feminist perspective. *Ecology Series*, 21. Heinrich Böll Stiftung, Berlin.
World Commission on Environment and Development (1987). *Our Common Future*. Oxford University Press.
Wright, M. (2010). Geography and gender: Feminism and a feeling of justice. *Progress in Human Geography*, *34*(6), 818–27.

Chapter 9

From Local Stories to Global Visions

> Too frequently we think we have to do spectacular things. Yet if we remember that the sea is actually made up of drops of water and each drop counts, each one of us can do our little bit where we are. Those little bits can come together and almost overwhelm the world. Each one of us can be an oasis of peace.
>
> —Desmond Tutu, South African theologian, recipient of the Nobel Peace Prize, 1984

From Local Stories to Global Visions

Malala Yousafzai was born in Pakistan on July 12' 1997. In 2008 when the Taliban took control, girls were no longer allowed to go to school and 11-year-old Malala had to say goodbye to her classmates and go home. In 2012, she spoke publicly about girls' right to education, and later that year a masked gunman attacked her and shot her in the head. She could have given up, but after two years of surgeries and rehabilitation, Malala chose to fight against injustice and established the Malala Fund to help girls get free, safe, quality education. In 2014 Malala became the youngest recipient of the Nobel Peace prize for her extraordinary courage. In 2020 she graduated from University of Oxford. She continues to help girls in many different countries achieve their dreams and holds leaders accountable for their promises. Malala is an inspiration to social justice activists around the world. We have much to learn from her.

Invitation to reflect: Take a moment to reflect on the courage that it took for Malala to stand up to the Taliban and demand the right to education for girls. What lessons can you learn from her actions?

Introduction

In chapter 8, we continued the work of developing a new vision by examining the interconnections between environmental crises and gender justice. We considered ways in which we can envision a more just and sustainable future. The feminist definition of development recognizes that we need to be better stewards of our natural resources and make choices that put the well-being of future generations and the long-term sustainability of our practices at the top of our list of priorities. This plan calls for transformative change by focusing on the synergies between sustainability and gender justice and putting care for all people and care for the planet front and center. The vision requires publicly funding universal care for all, sustainable livelihoods that work to reduce inequalities, especially gender inequalities, and sustainable consumption and production practices that reduce carbon emissions and create livable habitats for humans and other species. In this chapter we focus on how you and I working together can make this vision a reality. We will discuss how we can develop the ability to advocate and be agents of change for global justice and equity.

It is clear that the old social contract between governments and markets promising the dream and pronounced expectation of continuous economic growth and prosperity has fallen apart. As was discussed in earlier chapters, this dream was based on individualism, white supremacy, patriarchy, and unbridled profiteering, which led to a few getting rich on the backs of women, people of color, indigenous peoples, and the economically disadvantaged. It has led to widespread global fear and distrust. It has also led to the destruction of our environment to the point of near extinction, unless we change course now. We need a new feminist social contract. In the words of António Guterres, United Nations secretary-general (UN 2021, pg. 4)

> Now is the time to renew the social contract between Governments and their people and within societies, so as to rebuild trust and embrace a comprehensive vision of human rights. People need to see results reflected in their daily lives. This must include the active and equal participation of women and girls, without whom no meaningful social contract is possible.

Creating Spaces for Civic Engagement

The success of the feminist vision presented in earlier chapters requires strong democratic processes and a rethinking of the effectiveness of democratic institutions as they are currently situated, and instead encourage broad participation by all stakeholders, especially marginalized communities. Yet we seem to be moving in the opposite direction.

Civic Engagement During the Last Decade

According to UN Women (2021), 44% of people globally lived in countries that experienced an erosion in democracy between 2014 and 2019. According to the International Institute for Democracy and Electoral Assistance (International IDEA, 2019), this erosion of democracy is measured as declining freedom of expression, closing of public spaces, eroding rule of law, and increasing hate speech. Unfortunately, the lockdowns necessary during the pandemic led to the closure of public spaces for protests and other forms of assembly. It also led to curtailing of movement and postponement of elections, which further eroded democratic processes. The urgency created by crises has often meant the exclusion of women from decision-making processes (Herbert & Marquette, 2021). For example, out of the 225 COVID-19 task forces in 137 countries, 84% were dominated by men and 24 of them did not include a single woman. At the same time, women's organizations—especially those made up of marginalized women—mobilized very quickly and worked within their communities to provide care and food to those who didn't have social protections. The continuing pandemic has, however, taken a toll on these organizations as they continue to be underfunded and overworked.

Over the last few decades, rising inequality has concentrated political and economic power in the hands of a few, leading to an erosion of trust in public institutions and across social groups (Justino, 2015). Studies (Helliwell et al., 2021) have demonstrated that lower social trust is not only associated with lower well-being, but lower social trust is also associated with higher death rates due to COVID-19. Over the last several years, the anti-feminist movement has also gathered strength in many countries, and there have been rollbacks in policy commitments to gender equality. For example, Turkey withdrew from the Council of Europe Convention on Preventing and Combating Violence Against Women and Domestic Violence. The anti-women political rhetoric is often framed in terms of traditional family values arguing for women to return to the home and provide (unpaid) labor, which then allows for cutting social services. There has also been an erosion of women's reproductive rights, such as court rulings banning abortions in Poland in 2020 and court rulings rescinding women's right to an abortion in the United States in 2022.

Women's organizations have continued to protest after a brief drop in protests in early 2020. According to UN Women (2021), there were 5,012 demonstrations by women's organizations during the second half of 2020. These demonstrations have ranged from women demanding food aid and support for online schooling in Kazakhstan to calls for better working conditions for domestic workers in South Korea. Women's groups have also strongly resisted the rollback in women's rights. In Poland alone there were 617 women-led protests across the country in 2020. These movements have also formed broad coalitions with other social justice movements to support and strengthen each other. For example, in Brazil, women's organizations collaborated with organizations working for racial and economic justice and organizations working for LGBTQ rights to block as many as 76 regressive bills presented between 2015 and 2020 (Luna, 2019). In addition, several large protests known as the Feminist Spring in Brazil brought millions of women into the street. These included the Daisy March by rural women workers and the first Black Women's National March in 2015.

In several countries, feminist advocacy networks have been able to influence policy making. These countries include Argentina, Austria, Canada, Chile, Ireland, the United Kingdom, as well as Hawaii in the United States. For example, years of feminist advocacy in Argentina has led to gender balance in lower and upper legislative branches of government. Argentina also has a national level ministry of gender equality and gender equality divisions in several other ministries. They have a group called *Mujeres Gobernando* (Women Governing), composed of more than 150 cabinet ministers, lawmakers, and bureaucrats to incorporate a gender perspective into public policies. Street demonstrations by advocacy groups also maintained pressure on the government. As a result, when COVID-19 hit, they were able to put together a comprehensive package that included measures to address social protections, women's economic security, unpaid care work, and violence against women.

Moving Forward by Creating Spaces for Civic Engagement

Strong partnerships between the state, community organizations, and women's right groups are critical to

ensure accountability and solutions that are informed by those who are the hardest hit by crises. We need greater participation by women, especially indigenous women and women of color, at all levels of political decision-making. Studies have shown that in countries with more women legislators there tends to be higher spending on family friendly policies and lower spending on the military (O'Brien & Piscopo, 2019). The impact is even greater when these women legislators are connected to women's organizations and are able to ensure that the agenda is not watered down. Uruguay, Canada, and Argentina are great examples of how a large number of women legislators in key positions can be effective in turning the feminist agenda into policy. Having said that, we have a long way to go globally since women account for only 25% of those in parliament and 20% of ministers. In addition, most of these women tend to belong to the class privileged elite.

Women's organizations also play a critical role in turning the feminist agenda into policy (Htun & Weldon, 2018). These organizations need to be adequately funded and supported in the work that they do to ensure long-term sustainability, but also to ensure that we don't exploit women's unpaid community work. We need to create space for them to formally collaborate with the government on policymaking, implementing, and monitoring quality and accessibility of services. Marginalized communities are far more likely to trust and work with state bureaucracies when women's organizations have a formal role in the process (Evans et al., 2015). The Kudumbashree Mission established in the Indian state of Kerala in 1998 is a great example of community organizations and women's groups partnering with the state to help solve critical problems facing marginalized communities, especially women (Agarwal, 2021). Early in the pandemic, the Kudumbashree Mission was able to connect women's group farmers with food kitchens to provide food security for migrant workers (Kudumbashree, 2020). Over the years, the Mission has been able to nurture political participation by women, and many of them have become elected officials, creating further support for the agenda of women's groups.

Another important organizing principle is to recognize that one size does not fit all. We should not fall into the same trap that many developmental economists fell into by recommending the same economic model for all. It is important to follow the lead of local and indigenous peoples in the search for solutions that work within that local context, while at the same time recognizing that we are all connected and affected by global processes and interactions (Mohanty, 2003). As Mohanty (2013) points out, a dominant narrative can often marginalize the voices of the people that have the lived experiences and knowledge of the specific contexts within which their oppression is occurring. Any solutions proffered without knowledge of specific contexts are meaningless and ultimately will perpetuate injustices.

We can learn from a positive example in Uganda, where women's organizations organized a Women's Peace Caravan in 2006. They traveled across the country to demand a role in the peace negotiations that were underway between the LRA (Lord's Resistance Army) and the Ugandan government. Women had suffered the most from the conflict, and after 19 years of conflict, they demanded accountability and commitment to peace from all actors.

Another example we can learn from is in Brazil where mass social movements in the 1980s used Freire's model of liberatory education to develop social movement education modules that were offered throughout the country, especially to those without access to resources. The module started with a reflection on one's own lived experiences, followed by identification of problems and skill development to solve the problem, followed by action. As shared by Needleman (2011) this education opportunity was provided to a group of women *quilombeiras* who are descendants of African women brought to Brazil as slaves. They had carried African rice seeds with them hidden in their hair. They escaped from the plantations and established their own marooned communities with African rice ultimately being their major source of sustenance. While participating in the social movement education module, they learned about the nutritional value of the rice they cultivated, and they decided to use sustainable practices to expand cultivation of African rice, form a cooperative, and sell their rice to support themselves and their families.

A third example includes RAWA, the Revolutionary Association of the Women of Afghanistan, which was established in 1977. Their founder, Meena, was assassinated in 1987, at which time they became a mostly underground resistance movement, fighting for human rights and social justice through education and political resistance without violence. According to their mission, "*Whenever fundamentalists exist as a military and political force in our injured land, the problem of Afghanistan will not be solved. Today RAWA's mission for women's rights is far from over and we have to work hard for establishment of an independent, free, democratic and secular Afghanistan.*" In addition to their political resistance efforts, their programs include medical care facilities, education programs, orphanages, reconstruction, food aid, and emergency services. Their membership is restricted to Afghan women, although they encourage Afghan male supporters as well as transnational male and female supporters. This rule allows them to maintain female leadership and local autonomy over their activities and mission (Fluri, 2011).

All three of these examples highlight the importance of education in understanding the nature of the oppression. They also highlight the need for local communities to have the autonomy and support to identify local solutions that work for their particular circumstances. Challenging social injustice takes courage, and working in community emboldens and strengthens our resolve and persistence in the face of adversity and violence.

It is also important to build coalitions transnationally, recognizing our interdependence and membership in each other's lives. While digital technologies have made it easier to build transnational coalitions, it is also important to pay attention to global inequalities in access to digital technologies and work to eliminate them. It is critical that these partnerships and coalitions are entered into as equals so that the voices of local women don't get co-opted by more powerful voices. For example, Palestinian feminist scholar/activist Islah Jad (2007) points out that the Palestinian women's movement that was focused on gender and national liberation was co-opted by NGOs (non-governmental organizations) who were focused on peace negotiations between Israeli and Palestinian women.

It is also important that transnational support respect the knowledge and autonomy of local women to understand, prioritize, and identify solutions that work for them. Without this respect, transnational support might make the situation worse. For example, in Nigeria in 2002, Amina Lawal Kurami was sentenced to death by stoning for alleged adultery. In an effort to free her, several transnational organizations circulated petitions. In these petitions Africa and Islam were depicted as barbaric, which was not only a misrepresentation of the problem but also demonstrated the NGO's arrogance and ignorance of the realities and efforts of local Nigerian women's organizations. It also homogenized the experiences of women in different parts of the world, erasing the specific context and lived experiences of these women. Some international organizations, such as the International Association of Women Judges (IAWJ), listened to Nigerian activists and helped raise funds to cover legal costs versus signing petitions. In other words, we should not pull back transnational support for our sisters (who are fighting for justice in different parts of the world) because we are afraid of getting it wrong (Tripp, 2011). Instead, we should ask them with humility and compassion how they would like to be helped and follow their lead.

Creating Communities for Compassionate Action

As we come to the end of this book, you might be asking what you can do to contribute toward a more just and compassionate world. In the words of African American author Ruth King (2018),

> As you become more mindful ... there is a social responsibility you can't escape. For example, if you are doing harm, you feel the need to put a stop to it. If you see someone else doing harm, you feel the need to stop them. If you see systems at work that harm others or that harm the planet, you feel the need to join with others to make sure the harm stops. When you don't act you are an accomplice to injustice.

Invitation to reflect: Take a moment to reflect on a time when you (or someone you know) did not take action to stop acts of injustice. How did it make you feel? If you are in that situation again, is there anything you would do differently?

We must start by believing that we are capable of transforming the world even when we are faced with injustices that seem relentless in their scope, their historical underpinnings, their longevity, and their ability to continually shift and morph into new forms of injustice. It can be exhausting and discouraging, and it is important to take the time to rejuvenate, rest, and reconnect with our *deepest intention* and with each other with kindness and compassion. Recently, at the end of a long semester, the Center for Contemplative Practices at my university, of which I am a part, offered a day-long workshop on reconnecting with our deepest intentions. One of the practices involved looking deep inside yourself and asking why am I here? As I dug deeper into my inner self, the image that arose again and again in my mind was that of my daughter, and I realized that my deepest intention was to help build a more just and compassionate world for her and for all our children around the world. In order to do that effectively, I need to replenish my inner resources so I can find the courage and strength to keep going even when it seems impossible.

Invitation to reflect: Take a moment to reflect on why am I here and what is my deepest intention?

Role of Education and Awareness

The first step toward transforming the world is to develop awareness and understanding of the factors that create and perpetuate social injustices. Engaging with the material in this book is one way of developing awareness. There are many other books, documentaries, courses, testimonies, and the lived experiences of ourselves and those of others that can help build awareness and understanding (Combahee River Collective, 1986). **Inspired by Freire's work, Barbara Love (2000) puts forward the notion of "liberatory consciousness" as the process that an individual might go through from awareness to analysis to action.** Harro's concept of the cycle of liberation (2000) suggests that people have to change through a process of introspection, reflection, and educating oneself about the causes and consequences of social injustices. Growing awareness will manifest itself in the way that we interact with others. We will learn to acknowledge each other's humanity, treat each other with respect, and listen to each other with kindness and compassion. It is important for us to interact with people who are like us *and* with people who are not like us in terms of social identities.

The self-reflection must also include our willingness to examine our own privilege and complicity in the oppression of others along one or more of the many social identities we inhabit. We might often be blind to our own privilege. When it becomes visible to us for the first time, it can often bring denial, anger, guilt, confusion, and other painful emotions. But by recognizing the harm that such systems of oppression cause to those who are oppressed, we can choose to return to our deepest intention. For example, those of us who live in the global North with relative economic privilege might reflect on our own consumption patterns and the impact that these consumption patterns have on the rest of the planet, especially those with the least access to economic resources. When we learn, as we did in chapter 8, that our current pattern of consumption will make the habitat of billions of humans and millions of other species unlivable, our reaction might be to act out of fear. We might build walls and hoard resources to protect ourselves from the inevitable migration flows such habitat destruction will cause. Instead, we can learn to respond with compassion by changing our consumption patterns now and preventing potentially devastating outcomes for our fellow human beings and ourselves, for both current and future generations. We can create communities of compassionate action and educate and support each other in this work, especially when it gets difficult. We can hold ourselves and the suffering of others around the world in compassion as we learn to expand our hearts and our notions of family and belonging. In the words of Dr. Martin Luther King Jr. (1967), "*Power without love is reckless and abusive, and love without power is sentimental and anemic. Power at its best is love implementing the demands of justice, and justice at its best is love correcting everything that stands against love.*"

Love (2000) encourages us to envision the world we want to live in or the world we want our children to live in. It is important to stand *for* something versus only fighting against something. We need to fight against social injustice, but we also need to think about what a socially just world would look and feel like so we can aspire toward it. This vision could be broad, or it could be very specific. In earlier chapters we have discussed the feminist vision in terms of principles and broad conceptualizations. When we get to the implementation phase, it is imperative that we think about how our actions can reflect the world we want to live in and leave for our children. We also need to think about how we advocate for social justice without causing more hurt and harm. Finally, we need to think about how this broad vision could work in the specific context of the local environment we live in with its constraints and possibilities. For example, in chapter 6 we talked about gender and other inequities that exist in the care economy. Within our communities of compassionate action, we might take the time to listen to each other's stories and dreams about how we would like the care economy to work. We would find common ground, but we would also find vast differences. For example, we might have aging parents that we worry about, but my options for care might be very different from yours. As a community, we would work to develop our capacity for compassion and our ability to listen to those with the least access to resources and then follow their lead in developing a vision of how we might address these inequalities so that everyone's care needs are met.

From Vision to Action

Going from vision to action requires an awareness of where each community is in their own process of becoming agents of change. Adams and Bell (2016) identify several points on an action continuum ranging from actively participating in oppression to actively resisting it. The process of becoming agents of change involves being able to progressively move along the continuum below, which is adapted from Adams and Bell (2016).

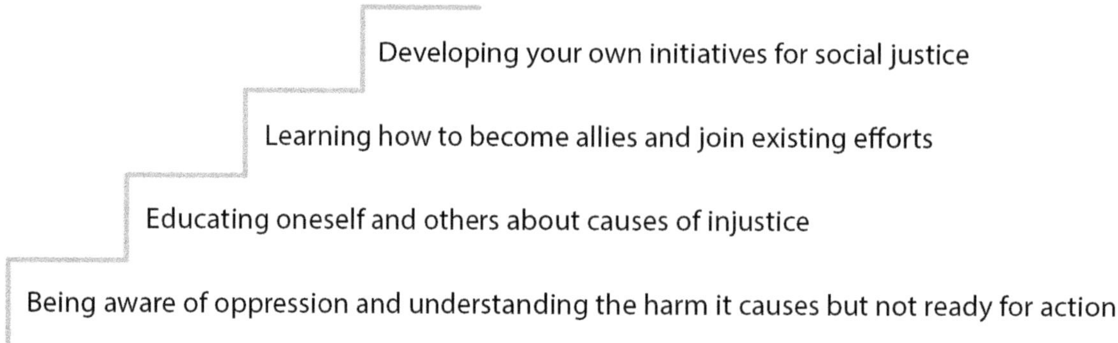

Image 9.1

As communities for compassionate action develop, they might be at various stages in the process. Along the continuum there will be groups who are aware of oppression and understand the harm that it causes, but they have not yet got to the point of action. Perhaps they are not sure what action to take or find that they don't have time to engage in action. Then there are those who are taking action, such as educating themselves and others and learning more so they can dismantle unjust structures. At this stage, it is important to engage in critical analysis of the factors that are causing and perpetuating oppression, to include multiple perspectives, and to have dialog and discussion with other groups. At the next stage, there are those who are learning how to become responsible allies and joining existing movements or actions to dismantle oppressive structures. Finally, there are those who are full-fledged activists coming up with their own ideas of resistance, making sure that voices of the oppressed are included in their work.

Invitation to reflect: Take a moment to reflect on a time when you (or someone you know) took action to stop acts of injustice. How did it make you feel? What was the outcome? If you could take action again, is there anything you would change?

Planning for action also involves identifying the outcomes, clear timelines, potential collaborators, barriers, and spheres of influence. **Spheres of influence might include your friends and family, institutional (working within an existing organization), or social (larger community of people).** Another way to think about it is whether the action you plan to take is for you individually, such as educating yourself or changing your behavior in some way. Some examples might include reducing or changing consumption patterns to lower carbon emissions or men taking on more care responsibilities in the home and the workplace. The action could also involve networking with others, such as educating others or creating an awareness campaign or planning an action together. These actions could include supporting legislative bills that provide care services for all or providing care services in your workplace or in your home for domestic workers. The action could also be about building coalitions with other groups or organizations toward common goals.

Building Coalitions

The next step is to start building coalitions so as to collaborate and act together to bring about change. As we have discussed in earlier chapters, different forms of injustices work together to reinforce, perpetuate, and amplify oppression. Therefore, it is not enough to focus on one form of oppression and assume that the other ones don't matter. They all do! It is in all our interest to work together and build coalitions across diverse groups. We are stronger when we work together. We are able to gain multiple perspectives and insights from the lived experiences of different groups, experiences that no one group can claim to have. It is easy to become singularly focused on one's own oppression and discount that of others. When we do that, we are only strengthening the interconnected power structures that rely on our division (Crenshaw, 1991). It is important to learn to listen to each other with compassion as much as it is important to share our own insights and stories. Building thoughtful and strategic coalitions requires searching for and agreeing on a set of common goals even if there are other areas of dissonance. This process can be facilitated by mindful communication, which requires compassionate listening and sharing with the intent of increasing mutual understanding and reducing suffering (Thich Nhat Hanh, 2014). As mentioned earlier, members of dominant groups must engage in self-reflection and acknowledge their privilege before they can engage with and be allies in the movement for social justice.

Invitation to reflect: Take a moment to reflect on one action you can take to work more closely with people "different" from you (i.e., people with different social identities) in order to bring about social justice.

In closing, I have often reflected on how I can best contribute toward building a more just and compassionate world, and the answer in some form or the other has always come back to my role as a teacher/scholar. Students come to the university so that they can have a transformative educational experience: so that they can transform their lives and the world that they live in. The rest of us are here to help our students have that transformative experience. It is our job as educators, parents, and loved ones to bring out the best in our students by always believing in them and by always being able to see potential in them that they might not see in themselves. We teach so that students can learn about the complex causes of social injustice. We question so that students can seek answers that work for them. We care so that students learn how to love. We breathe so that students can learn how to live in a future that we will not be part of because in the words of Khalil Gibran, "they dwell in the house of tomorrow which I cannot visit even in my dreams."

I would like to share with you one of my favorite poems from my childhood. It was written by Nobel laureate Rabindranath Tagore (1912). He wrote it before India's independence in 1947, and this is what he wished for his country. He wrote the following:

Where the mind is without fear and the head is held high

Where knowledge is free

Where the world has not been broken up into fragments

By narrow domestic walls

Where words come out from the depth of truth

Where tireless striving stretches its arms towards perfection

Where the clear stream of reason has not lost its way

Into the dreary desert sand of dead habit

Where the mind is led forward by thee

Into ever-widening thought and action

Into that heaven of freedom, my Father, let my country awake

(Rabindranath Tagore, "Gitanjali 35," *Gitanjali*, Macmillan, 1913.)

This is my dream, my hope for the whole world, that our minds are without fear and our heads are held high. I hope that engaging with the content of this book has inspired us to open our minds and our hearts without fear. I hope that we have learned to combine wisdom with love and insight with compassion. Above all else, I hope that we have learned a bit more how to love—to love each other and this amazing planet that we share—and become inspired to love the world enough to assume responsibility for it.

As we grapple with a global pandemic, climate change, and increasing inequality and we ask ourselves who gets to have shelter, who gets to have food, who gets to receive care, who gets to have a voice, and who gets to thrive and survive, I hope our answer is we all do!

Key Takeaways

Below are the key ideas to take away from this chapter:

- It is clear that the old social contract between governments and markets promising the dream of economic growth and prosperity has fallen apart. We need a new feminist social contract.
- The success of the feminist vision presented in earlier chapters requires strong democratic processes that encourage broad based participation by all stakeholders, especially marginalized communities.
- Strong partnerships between the state, community organizations, and women's right groups are critical to ensure accountability and solutions that are informed by those who are the hardest hit by crises. We need greater participation by women, especially indigenous women and women of color,

at all levels of political decision-making.

- It is important to recognize that one size does not fit all. It is important to follow the lead of local and indigenous peoples in the search for solutions that work within that local context while at the same time recognizing that we are all connected and affected by global processes and interactions.
- The first step toward transforming the world is for people to change through a process of introspection, reflection, and educating oneself about the causes and consequences of social injustices.
- We can create communities of compassionate action and educate and support each other in this work, especially when it gets difficult as it inevitably will. We can hold ourselves and the suffering of others around the world in compassion as we learn to expand our hearts and our notions of family and belonging.

Comprehension Questions

Directions: Use what you have learned in this chapter to help you respond to the questions below:

1. Why do we need strong democratic processes to achieve the feminist vision presented in earlier chapters?
2. What is the role that women's organizations play in turning feminist agenda into action?
3. Why is it important to create space for civic engagement at the local level?
4. How can communities for compassionate action help contribute to achieving the feminist vision presented in earlier chapters?

References

Adams, M., & Bell, L. (2016). *Teaching for Diversity and Social Justice* (3rd ed.), Routledge.

Agarwal, B. (2021). Livelihoods in COVID times: Gendered perils and new pathways in India. *World Development,* 139, 1–7.

Combahee River Collective. (1986). *The Combahee River Collective Statement: Black Feminist Organizing in the Seventies and Eighties.* Latham, NY: Kitchen Table, Women of Color Press.

Crenshaw, K. (1991). Mapping the margins: Intersectionality, identity politics and violence against women of color. *Stanford Law Review,* 43(6), 1241–1299.

Evans, P., Huber, E., & Stephens, J. (2015). *The political foundations of state effectiveness.* Working Paper No. 24. The Watson Institute for International Studies, Brown University, Providence, RI.

Fluri, J. (2011). Feminist nation building in Afghanistan: An examination of the Revolutionary Association of the Women in Afghanistan (RAWA). In N. Visvanathan, L. Duggan, N. Wiegersma, & L. Nisonoff (Eds.). *The Women, Gender and Development Reader* (2nd ed.). Zed Books.

Harro, B. (2000). The cycle of liberation. In M. Adams, W. Blumenfeld, C. R. Casteñeda, H. W. Hackman, M. L. Peters, & X. Zuniga (Eds.), Readings for Diversity and Social Justice. New York: Routledge.

Helliwell, J., Huang, H., Wang, S., & Norton, M. (2021). World happiness, trust and deaths under COVID 19. In *World Happiness Report 2021 (chapter 2).*

Herbert, S., & Marquette, H. (2021). COVID-19, governance, and conflict: Emerging impacts and future evidence needs. K4D Emerging Issues Report 34. Institute of Development Studies, Brighton, UK.

Htun, M., & Weldon, S. (2018). The Logics of Gender Justice. Cambridge University Press.

International IDEA (Institute for Democracy and Electoral Assistance). (2019). The Global State of Democracy 2019: Addressing the Ills, Reviving the Promise. Stockholm: International IDEA.

Jad, I. (2007). NGOs: Between buzzwords and social movements. *Development in Practice,* 17(4–5), 622–29.

Justino, P. (2015). *Inequality, social cooperation and local collective action.* IDS Working Paper 457. Institute for Development Studies (IDS), Brighton, UK.

>King, M., Jr. (1967). Where Do We Go From Here? Annual Report Delivered at the 11th Convention of the Southern Christian Leadership Conference, August 16, Atlanta, GA.
King, R. (2018). *Mindful of Race.* Sounds True, Boulder, Colorado.
Kudumbashree. (2020). *Brief study on COVID-19 pandemic and its economic impacts on farm livelihood (JLGS) of Kudumbashree.* Kudumbashree State Mission, Thiruvananthapuram, India.
Love, B. (2000). Developing a Liberatory Consciousness. In M. Adams, W. Blumenfeld, R. Castaneda, H. Hackman, M. Peters & X. Zuniga (Eds.). Readings for Diversity and Social Justice. Routledge: New York.
Luna, N. (2019). Debate Sobre Aborto Na Camara de Deputados No Brasil Entre 2015 e 2017: Agenda conservadora e resistencia. *Sexualidad, Salud y Sociedad,* 33, 207–239.
Mohanty, C. (2003). *Feminism Without Borders: Decolonizing Theory, Practicing Solidarity.* Duke University Press.
Mohanty, C. (2013). Transnational feminist crossings: On neoliberalism and radical critique. *Signs: Journal of Women in Culture and Society,* 38(4), 967–991.
Needleman, R. (2011). 'I am somebody': Brazil's social movements educate for gender equality and economic sustainability. In N. Visvanathan, L. Duggan, N. Wiegersma, & L. Nisonoff (Eds.). *The Women, Gender and Development Reader* (2nd ed.). Zed Books.
O'Brien, D. & Piscopo, J. (2019). The Impact of Women in Parliament. In S. Franceschet, M. Krook & N. Tan (Eds.). The Palgrave Handbook of Women's Political Rights. Palgrave McMillan.
Tagore, R. (1912). Gitanjali. India Society in London.
Thich Nhat Hanh. (2014). *The Art of Communicating.* HarperCollins Publishers.
Tripp, A. (2011). Challenges in transnational feminist mobilization. In N. Visvanathan, L. Duggan, N. Wiegersma, & L. Nisonoff (Eds.). *The Women, Gender and Development Reader* (2nd ed.). Zed Books.
UN (2021). Our Common Agenda – Report of the Secretary-General. United Nations: New York.
UN Women (2021) *Beyond Covid-19: A feminist plan for sustainability and social justice.* Research and Data Section, UN Women.

www.ingramcontent.com/pod-product-compliance
Ingram Content Group UK Ltd.
Pitfield, Milton Keynes, MK11 3LW, UK
UKHW051452290926
15471UKWH00008B/1171

9 781793 556714